LETTERS OF TRANSIT

Letters
of Transit

REFLECTIONS ON EXILE,
IDENTITY, LANGUAGE,
AND LOSS

Edited by André Aciman

*Published in collaboration with
The New York Public Library*

THE NEW PRESS
NEW YORK

The lecture series "Letters of Transit" was conceived and
coordinated by André Aciman and presented by the Public
Education Program of The New York Public Library's Humanities
and Social Sciences Library, Fifth Avenue and 42nd Street,
New York, N.Y., September 1997–February 1998.

Published in the United States by The New Press, New York
Distributed by W. W. Norton & Company, Inc., New York

The New Press was established in 1990 as a not-for-profit alternative
to the large, commercial publishing houses currently dominating
the book publishing industry. The New Press operates in the public
interest rather than for private gain, and is committed to publishing,
in innovative ways, works of educational, cultural, and community
value that are often deemed insufficiently profitable.

www.thenewpress.com

BOOK DESIGN BY ANN ANTOSHAK

PRINTED IN THE UNITED STATES OF AMERICA

9 8 7 6 5 4 3 2 1

Contents

Permanent Transients

André Aciman

What does it mean to be an exile? How does exile alter someone? How does it reinvent one? What *is* exile? When does it go away? Does it ever go away? What is the difference between, say, a refugee and an expatriate, or between an immigrant and an emigrant, or between the uprooted and the unrooted, the displaced, the *dépaysés,* the evicted, the *émigrés?*—people who didn't just lift themselves up with their roots but who may have no roots left at all? These are the issues each of the five authors gathered here has tried to address in these essays originally delivered in The New York Public Library's lecture series "Letters of Transit."

Everyone's exile is different, and every writer has his or her own way of groping in the dark. Some have triumphed over exile. Others even found displacement exciting, invigorating. Others were able to don it and doff it, like a costume, while others have never been able to shake it off. But exile, however exiles deal with it, is never far behind, whether we're talking of a Yugoslavian in exile (Charles Simic), or a Bengali in exile (Bharati Mukherjee), or a Pole in exile (Eva Hoffman), or a Palestinian in exile (Edward Said), or an

Alexandrian in exile (André Aciman). Each one of the writers here writes from overt, or, more frequently, covert homesickness—tales of memory, loss, fear, anger, inevitable acculturation, muffled irony in the face of self-pity, and final redemption in this strange and often sorely unnatural thing called naturalization. Having chosen careers in writing, each uses the written word as a way of fashioning a new home elsewhere, of revisiting, transposing, or perpetuating the old one on paper, writing away the past the way one writes off bad debts, doing the one absurd thing all exiles do, which is to look for their homeland abroad, or to try to restore it abroad, or, more radical yet, to dispose of it abroad. However successful the endeavor is by the end of the day, the same perplexities, the same homesickness stirs to life again the next morning.

What makes exile the pernicious thing it is is not really the state of being away, as much as the impossibility of ever *not* being away—not just being absent, but never being able to redeem this absence. You look back on your life and find your exile announced everywhere, from events shaped as far back as the Congress of Vienna in 1815 down to the fact that, for some fortuitous reason, your parents decided to make certain you learned English as a child. Bewildered by narratives that pullulate everywhere he looks, an exile has yet to answer a far more fundamental question: in what language will he express his confused awareness of these intimate paradoxes?

Paradoxically enough, the answer in these five cases is English—the foreign tongue.

Five voices, five tales, five worlds, five lives that might have little in common but for the fact that none of the foreign-born authors gathered in this volume is a native speaker of English. English, for all five, is an acquired language, a foreign idiom, and it remains, perhaps against their will and more than they care to own, alien, strange, distant. After many decades in the United States, or Canada, or England, most still speak English with an accent, as though an accent didn't betray just the body's inability to adapt or to square away the details of a naturalization that should have been finalized decades ago, but its reluctance to let go of things that are at once private and timeless, the way childhood and ritual and memory are private and timeless. Some of the writers still make out traces of an accent in their own prose, call it a particular cadence in a language that is never quite just English but not anything else either. An accent is the tell-tale scar left by the unfinished struggle to acquire a new language. But it is much more.

It is an author's way of compromising with a world that is not his world and for which he was not and, in a strange sense, will never be prepared, torn as he'll always remain between a new, thoroughly functional here-and-now and an old, competing altogether-out-there that continues to exert a vestigial but enduring pull. An accent marks the lag between two cultures, two languages, the space where you let go of one identity, invent another, and end up being more than one person though never quite two.

Yet all five of these authors are so thoroughly at home—*rooted* might be the more appropriate, if ironic, term—in English that it is difficult to remember they come from an entirely different hemisphere. English has become the language they speak at home. They write almost exclusively in English, and ultimately count, sing, cook, quarrel, and dream in English. Those of them who have children have tried to pass on the ur-language with varying degrees of success. But the ur-anything pales when it comes to report cards, baseball practice, television, college applications, careers. English is the everyday, nuts-and-bolts language. It may not be the language of the heart, the language of grief and gossip and good-night kisses; but all of these authors write in English when they write from the heart.

Every successful sentence they write reminds them that they've probably made it to safety. It is, after all, a source of no small satisfaction to be mistaken for a native speaker. Theirs, however, is the satisfaction that men like Demosthenes and Moses might have felt on telling their closest admirers that what turned them to public speaking was not the power of their beliefs but something as trivial as a speech defect. Foreigners frequently master the grammar of a language better than its native speakers, the better, perhaps, to hide their difference, their diffidence, which also explains why they are so tactful, almost ceremonial, when it comes to the language they adopt, bowing before its splendor, its arcane syntax, to say nothing of its slang, which they use sparingly, and somewhat stiffly, with the studied nonchalance of people who aren't confident enough to dress down when the need arises.

Eventually, of course, one does stop being an exile. But even a "reformed" exile will continue to practice the one thing exiles do almost as a matter of instinct: compulsive retrospection. With their memories perpetually on overload, exiles see double, feel double, are double. When exiles see one place they're also seeing—or looking for—another behind it. Everything bears two faces, everything is shifty because everything is mobile, the point being that exile, like love, is not just a condition of pain, it's a condition of deceit.

Or put it another way: exiles can be supremely mobile, and they can be totally dislodged from their original orbit, but in this jittery state of transience, they are thoroughly stationary—no less stationary than those displaced Europeans perpetually awaiting letters of transit in the film *Casablanca*. They are never really in Casablanca, but they are not going anywhere either. They are in permanent transience.

Exiles see two or more places at the same time not just because they're addicted to a lost past. There is a very real, active component to seeing in this particularly heightened retrospective manner: an exile is continuously prospecting for a future home—forever looking at alien land as land that could conceivably become his. Except that he does not stop shopping for a home once he's acquired one or once he's finally divested himself of exile. He goes on prospecting, partly because he cannot have the home he remembers and partly because his new home bears no relationship to the old. Over and above these minor distinctions, however, his problem starts at home, with home. There isn't—and, in certain cases, wasn't —any.

The question our five writers ask is how do you—indeed, can you ever—rebuild a home? What kinds of shifts must take place for a person to acquire, let alone accept, a new identity, a new language? The answers are different, not just because their voices and concerns are different, but because the psychological raw material which each author brings to the puzzle is different as well. Still, here, in this volume, all five authors have shown us how each, in his or her way, has tried to make a home and refashion a life. Let's bear in mind that the next time we read them they won't be as forthcoming. Like friends who happened to open up one day only to withdraw afterwards, they'll be addressing a host of other issues, almost forgetting they showed us their deepest and most private side here.

Let's remember, then, that the words they'll be using won't just be English words jotted down in an effort to communicate with their English-speaking readers. Their words, despite their desire to appear so coolly collected and focused, are the priceless buoys with which they try to stay afloat both as professional thinkers and human beings.

Shadow Cities

André Aciman

Why spurn my home when exile is your home?
The Ithaca you want you'll have in not having.
You'll walk her shores yet long to tread those very grounds,
kiss Penelope yet wish you held your wife instead,
touch her flesh yet yearn for mine.
Your home's in the rubblehouse of time now,
and you're made thus, to yearn for what you lose.

FROM *Out of Egypt: A Memoir* (1994)

❧

On a late spring morning in New York City almost two years ago, while walking on Broadway, I suddenly noticed that something terrible had happened to Straus Park. The small park, located just where Broadway intersects West End Avenue on West 106th Street, was being fenced off. A group of workers, wearing orange reflector shins, were manning all kinds of equipment, and next to what must have been some sort of portable comfort station was a large electrical generator. Straus Park was being dismantled, demolished.

Not that Straus Park was such a wonderful place to begin with. Its wooden benches were dirty, rotting, and perennially littered with pigeon droppings. You'd think twice before sitting, and if you did sit you'd want to leave immediately. It had also become a favorite hangout for the homeless, the drunk, and the addicted. Over the years the old cobblestone pavement had turned into an undulating terrain of dents and bulges, mostly cracked, with missing pieces sporadically replaced by tar or cement, the whole thing blanketed by a deep, drab, dirty gray. Finally, the emptied basin of what used to be a fountain had turned into something resembling a septic sandbox. Unlike the fountains of Rome, this one, like the park itself, was a down-and-out affair. Never a drop flowed from it. The fountain had been turned off decades ago.

Straus Park was, like so many tiny, grubby parks one hardly ever notices on the Lower East Side, a relic of a past that wasn't ancient enough to have its blemishes forgiven or to feel nostalgic about. One could say the same of the Art Nouveau-style statue of what I took to be a reclining Greek nymph lost in silent contemplation, looking inward, as it were, to avoid looking at what was around her. She looked very innocent, very Old World, and very out of place, almost pleading to be rescued from this ugly shrub that dubbed itself a park. In fact, the statue wasn't even there that day. She had disappeared, no doubt sold.

The thing I liked most about the square was gone, the way so many other things are gone today from around Straus Park: the Olympia Deli, the Blue Rose, Ideal Restaurant, Mr. Kay's Barbershop, the Pomander Bookshop, the Siam Spice Rack, Chelsea Two, and the old Olympia Theater, drawn and quartered, as all the theaters are these days, plus the liquor store that moved across the street but really disappeared when it changed owners, the flower store that went high-tech, and La Rosita, which went from being down-and-out to up-and-coming.

Why should anybody care? And why should I, a foreigner, of all people care? This wasn't even my city. Yet I had come here, an exile from Alexandria, doing what

all exiles do on impulse, which is to look for their homeland abroad, to bridge the things here to things there, to
rewrite the present so as not to write off the past. I wanted to rescue things everywhere, as though by restoring
them here I might restore them elsewhere as well. In
seeing one Greek restaurant disappear or an old Italian
cobbler's turn into a bodega, I was once again reminded
that something was being taken away from the city and,
therefore, from me—that even if I don't disappear from
a place, places disappear from me.

I wanted everything to remain the same. Because
this too is typical of people who have lost everything,
including their roots or their ability to grow new ones.
It is precisely because you have no roots that you don't
budge, that you fear change, that you'll build on anything rather than look for land. An exile is not just
someone who has lost his home; it is someone who
can't find another, who can't think of another. Some
no longer even know what home means. They reinvent the concept with what they've got, the way we
reinvent love with what's left of it each time. Some
people bring exile with them the way they bring it
upon themselves wherever they go.

I hate it when stores change names, the way I hate
any change of season, not because I like winter more
than spring, or because I like old store X better than
new store Y, but because, like all foreigners who settle
here, and who always have the sense that their time
warp is not perfectly aligned to the city's, and that
they've docked, as it were, a few minutes ahead or a

few minutes behind Earth time, any change reminds me of how imperfectly I've connected to it. It reminds me of the thing I fear most: that my feet are never quite solidly on the ground, but also that the soil under me is equally weak, that the graft didn't take. In the disappearance of small things, I read the tokens of my own dislocation, of my own transiency. An exile reads change the way he reads time, memory, self, love, fear, beauty: in the key of loss.

I remembered that on summer days many years earlier when I was doing research on my dissertation, I would sometimes leave the gloomy stacks of Butler Library at Columbia and walk out into the sun down to 106th Street, where I'd find a secluded, shaded bench away from the drunks and sit there a while, eat a sandwich, a pizza, occasionally smiling at some of the elderly ladies who sat, not in the park, but along the benches outside, the way they did on Saturday afternoons around Verdi Square on 72nd Street and had probably learned to do on sunny, windy summer days in Central Europe, and as they still do in those mock-England spots in Paris that the French call *petits squares*, where people chat while their children play. Some of these ladies spoke with thick accents. I pictured their homes to myself, lots of lace, many doilies, Old World silverware, mannered Austro-Hungarian everything, down to the old gramophone, the black-and-white pictures on the wall, and de rigueur schnapps and slivovitz. They made me think of old 1950s pictures of a New York where it seemed to grow darker much sooner in the evening than it does nowadays, where everyone wore long gray overcoats because winters were always colder then, and of a time when the Upper West Side teemed with people who had come from Europe before the war and then stayed on, building small, cluttered lives, turning this neighborhood into a reliquary of Frankfurt-am-Main—their Frankfurt-away-from-home, Frankfurt-on-the-Hudson, as the old joke goes, but not an inappropriate reference to a city which, in Germany today, dubs itself Mainhattan, and which is, ironically enough, a far stranger city to them, now that it imitates Manhattan, than their adopted Manhattan imitating old Frankfurt.

There I met old Mrs. Danziger with the tattoo on her arm. Eighty-three-year-old Kurt Appelbaum, a concert pianist in his day, was sitting on such a bench; we spoke; we became friendly; one night, without my asking, he offered to play the Waldstein and the *Rhapsody in Blue* for me, "But do not tape," he said, perhaps because he wished I would, and now that I think of it, I wish I had, as I sat and listened on a broken chair he said had been given to him by Hannah Arendt, who had inherited it from an old German colleague at the New School who had since died as well.

That was the year I rediscovered the Busch Quartet's 1930s recordings of Beethoven, and I imagined its members playing everywhere in those Old World, prewar living rooms around Straus Park. And by force of visualizing them there, I projected them onto the park as well, so that its benches and the statue and the surrounding buildings and stores were, like holy men, stigmatized by Beethoven's music as it was played by a group of exiles from Hitler's Reich.

I would come every noon, for the statue mostly, because she was, like me, willing to stand by in this halfway station called Straus Park. She reminded me of those statues one finds everywhere in Rome, springing on you from their niches in the evening when you least expect them.

It is difficult to explain what seclusion means when you find it on an island in the middle of Broadway, amid the roar of midday traffic. What I was looking for, and had indeed found quite by accident, was something that reminded me of an oasis—in the metaphorical sense, since this was a "dry" fountain—but an oasis of the soul, a place where, for no apparent reason, people stop on their various journeys elsewhere. Straus Park, it seemed, was created precisely for this, for contemplation, for restoration—in both its meanings—for retrospection, for finding oneself, for finding the center of things.

And, indeed, there was something physically central about Straus Park. This, after all, was where Broadway and West End Avenue intersected, and the park seemed almost like a raised hub on West 106th Street, leading to Riverside Park on one side and to Central Park on the other. Straus Park was not on one street but at the intersection of four. Suddenly, before

I knew why, I felt quite at home. I was in one place that had at least four addresses.

Here you could come, sit, and let your mind drift in four different directions: Broadway, which at this height had an unspecified Northern European cast; West End, decidedly Londonish; 107th, very quiet, very narrow, tucked away around the corner, reminded me of those deceptively humble alleys where one finds stately homes along the canals of Amsterdam. And 106th, as it descended toward Central Park, looked like the main alley of a small town on the Italian Riviera, where, after much trundling in the blinding light at noon as you take in the stagnant odor of fuel from the train station where you just got off, you finally approach a sort of cove, which you can't make out yet but which you know is there, hidden behind a thick row of Mediterranean pines, over which, if you really strain your eyes, you'll catch sight of the tops of striped beach umbrellas jutting beyond the trees, and beyond these, if you could just take a few steps closer, the sudden, spectacular blue of the sea.

To the west of Straus Park, however, the slice of Riverside and 106th had acquired a character that was strikingly Parisian, and with the fresh breeze which seemed to swell and subside all afternoon long, you sensed that behind the trees of Riverside Park, serene and silent flowed an elusive Seine, and beyond it, past the bridges that were to take you across, though you couldn't see any of it yet, was not the Hudson, not New Jersey, but the Left Bank—not the end of Manhattan, but the beginning of a whole bustling city waiting beyond the trees—as it waited so many decades ago when, as a boy, dreaming of Paris, I would go to the window, look out to the sea at night, and think that this was not North Africa at all, but the Ile de la Cité. Perhaps what lay beyond the trees was not the end of Manhattan, or even Paris, but the beginnings of another, unknown city, the real city, the one that always beckons, the one we invent each time and may never see and fear we've begun to forget.

There were moments when, despite the buses and the trucks and the noise of people with boom boxes, the traffic light would change and everything came to a standstill and people weren't speaking, and the unrelenting sun beat strong on the pavement, and I would almost swear this was an early summer afternoon in Italy, and that what lay behind Riverside Park was not just my imaginary Seine, but the Tiber as well. What made me think of Rome was that everything here reminded me of the kind of place all tourists know well: that tiny, empty piazza with a little fountain, where, thirsty and tired with too much walking all day, you douse your face, then unbuckle your sandals, sit on the scalding marble edge of a Baroque fountain, and simply let your feet rest a while in what is always exquisitely clear, non-drinkable water.

Depending on where I sat, or on which corner I moved to within the park, I could be in any of four or five countries and never for a second be in the one I couldn't avoid hearing, seeing, and smelling. This,

I think, is when I started to love, if love is the word for it, New York. I would return to Straus Park every day, because returning was itself now part of the ritual of remembering the shadow cities hidden there—so that I, who had put myself there, the way squatters put themselves somewhere and start to build on nothing, with nothing, would return for no reason other than perhaps to run into my own footprints. This became my habit, and ultimately my habitat. Sometimes finding that you are lost where you were lost last year can be oddly reassuring, almost familiar. You may never find yourself; but you do remember looking for yourself. That too can be reassuring, comforting.

On a hot summer day I came looking for water in a place where no water exists, the way dowsers do when they search for trapped, underground places, seeking out the ghost of water, its remanence. But the kind of water I was really looking for was not fountain water at all, Roman or otherwise. I remembered my disappointment in Rome years ago when, dunking my feet in the turtle fountain early one afternoon, it occurred to me that these surreptitious footbaths in the middle of an emptied Rome in August and all this yearning for sunlight, heat, and water amounted to nothing more than a poor man's simulated swim at the beaches of childhood, where water was indeed plentiful, and where all of the body could bathe, not just the toes.

At Straus Park, I had discovered the memory of water. Here I would come to remember not so much the beauty of the past as the beauty of remembering, realizing that just because we love to look back doesn't mean we love the things we look back on.

There is a large fountain in Rome at Piazza Navona, where four rivers of the world are represented: the Ganges, the Nile, the Plate, and the Danube. I knew it well, because it stood not far from a small bookstore where, years ago, as a teenager, I would go to purchase one Penguin book a week—a small, muggy, and sultry shop, from which I recall the sense of bliss on first coming out into the sun with a new book in my hand. As I surveyed these four rivers, which, was the question, do I splash my face in?

There is no frigate like a book, says Emily Dickinson. There is nothing I have loved more than to take a good book and sit somewhere in a quiet open spot in Rome with so many old things around me, open up to any page, and begin traveling back, sometimes, as when I read Lawrence Durrell and Cavafy, thinking of time—of all that retrospection, to quote Whitman—or eagerly looking forward to the New World, as when I learned to love Eliot and Pound. Does a place become one's home because this is where one read the greatest number of books about other places? Can I long for Rome when I am finally standing where I yearned to stand when I was once a young man in Rome?

All this, if it hadn't already, began to acquire absurd proportions when I realized that, during that dissertation summer of many years ago, I had applied for and gotten a job teaching in an American high school in Rome. So as I sat here in Straus Park, going through my usual pickup-sticks and cat's cradle of memories, I discovered something rather unique: I didn't want to go to Rome, not for a year, not for half a year, not even for a month, because it finally dawned on me that I didn't very much like Rome, nor did I really want to be in France, or Egypt for that matter—and though I certainly did not like New York any better, I rather enjoyed my Straus-Park-Italy and my Straus-Park-Paris much more, the way sometimes I like postcards and travel books better than the places they remind me of, art books better than paintings, recordings better than live performances, and fantasies more than the people I fantasize about— some of whom are not only destined to disappoint, but can't even be forgiven for standing in the way of the pictures we originally had of them. Once in Rome, I would most certainly long to be in Straus Park remembering the Rome where I'd once remembered the beaches of my childhood. Italy was just my way of grafting myself onto New York.

I could never understand or appreciate New York unless I could make it the mirror—call it the mnemonic correlate—of other cities I've known or imagined. No Mediterranean can look at a sunset in Manhattan and not think of another sunset thousands of miles away. No Mediterranean can look at the tiny lights speckling the New Jersey cliffs at night and not remember a galaxy of little fishing boats that go out to sea at night, dotting the water with their tiny lights until dawn, when they come back to shore. It is not New Jersey I see when I watch the sun set from Riverside Drive.

The real New York I never see either. I see only the New York that either sits in for other places or helps me summon them up. New York is the stand-in, the ersatz of all the things I can remember and cannot have, and may not even want, much less love, but continue to look for, because finding parallels can be more compelling than finding a home, because without parallels, there can't be a home, even if in the end it is the comparing that we like, not the objects we compare. Outside of comparing, we cannot feel. One may falsify New York to make it more habitable; but by making it more habitable in that way one also makes certain that it remains a falsehood, a figment.

New York is my home precisely because it is a place from which I can begin to be elsewhere—an analogue city, a surrogate city, a shadow city that allows me to naturalize and neutralize this terrifying, devastating, unlivable megalopolis by letting me think it is something else, somewhere else, that it is indeed far smaller, quainter than I feared, the way certain cities on the Mediterranean are forever small and quaint, with just about the right number of places where people can go, sit, and, like Narcissus leaning over a pool of water, find themselves at every bend, every store window, every facade. Straus Park allowed me to place more than one film over the entire city of New York, the way certain guidebooks to Rome do. Along with each photograph of an ancient ruin comes a series of colored transparencies. When you place a transparency over the picture of the ruin, the missing or fallen parts suddenly reappear, showing you how the Forum and the Coliseum must have looked in their heyday, or how Rome looked in the Middle Ages, and then in the late Renaissance, and so on. But when you lift all the plastic sheets, all you see are today's ruins.

I didn't want to see the real New York. I'd go backward in time and uncover an older New York, as though New York, like so many other cities on the Mediterranean, had an ancient side that was less menacing, that was not so difficult to restore, that had more past than present, and that corresponded to the old-fashioned world I think I come from. Hence, my obsession with things that are old and defunct and that seep through like ancient cobblestones and buried rails from under renewed coats of asphalt and tar. Sealed-off ancient firehouses, ancient stables turned into garages, ghost buildings awaiting demolition, old movie theaters converted into Baptist churches, old marketplaces that are now lost, subway stops that are ghost stations today—these are the ruins I dream of restoring, if only to date the whole world back a bit to my time, the way Herr Appelbaum and Frau Danziger belonged to my time. Going to Straus Park was like traveling elsewhere in time. How frugal is the chariot that bears the human soul.

How uncannily appropriate, therefore, to find out fifteen years later that the statue that helped me step back in time was not that of a nymph, but of Memory herself. In Greek, her name is Mnemosyne, Zeus's mistress, mother of the Muses. I had, without knowing it, been coming to the right place after all. This is why I was so disturbed by the imminent demolition of the park: my house of memories would become a ghost park. If part of the city goes, part of us dies as well.

Of course, I had panicked too soon. Straus Park was marvelously restored. After spending more than a year in a foundry, a resurrected statue of Memory remembered her appointed place in the park and resumed her old position. Her fountain is the joy of children and of all the people who lean over to splash their faces on a warm summer day. I go there very often, sometimes to have coffee in the morning after dropping my children off at school. I have now forgotten what the old Straus Park looked like. I do not miss it, but somehow part of me is locked there too, so that I come here sometimes to remember my summer of many years ago as well, though I am glad those days are gone.

My repeated returns to Straus Park make of New York not only the shadow city of so many other cities I've known, but a shadow city of itself, reminding me of an earlier New York in my own life, and before that of a New York which existed before I was born and which has nothing to do with me but which I need to see—in old photographs, for example—because, as an exile without a past, I like to peek at others' foundations to imagine what mine might look like had I been born here, where mine might be if I were to build here. I like to know that Straus Park was once called Schuyler Square, and before that Bloomingdale Square, and that these are places where everything about me and the city claims a long, continuous, call it a common, ancestral, imaginary past, where nothing ever bolts into sudden being, but where nothing ever disappears, not those I love today, nor those I've loved in the past, that Old World people like Herr Appelbaum, who played Gershwin for me on 105th Street one night when he could have played Schubert instead, and Mrs. Danziger, who never escaped the Nazis but brought them with her in her dreams at night, might still sit side by side with Ida Straus, who refused to board the lifeboats when the *Titanic* sank and stayed on with her husband—that all these people and all these layers upon layers of histories, warmed-over memories, and overdrawn fantasies should forever go into letting my Straus Park, with its Parisian Frankfurts and Roman Londons, remain forever a tiny, artificial speck on the map of the world that is my center of gravity, from which radiates every road I've traveled, and to which I always long to return when I am away.

But perhaps I should spell the mystery out and say what lies at the bottom of all this. Straus Park, this crossroads of the world, this capital of memory, this place where the four fountains of the world and the four quarters within me meet one another, is not Paris, is not Rome, could not be London or Amsterdam, Frankfurt or New York. It is, of course, Alexandria.

I come to Straus Park to remember Alexandria, albeit an unreal Alexandria, an Alexandria that does not exist, that I've invented, or learned to cultivate in Rome as in Paris, so that in the end the Paris and the Rome I retrieve here are really the shadow of the shadow of Alexandria, versions of Alexandria, the remanence of Alexandria, infusing Straus Park itself now, reminding me of something that is not just elsewhere but that is perhaps more in me than it was ever out there, that it is, after all, perhaps just me, a me that is no less a figment of time than this city is a figment of space.

The New Nomads

Eva Hoffman

ᴗ

In *Speak, Memory,* Nabokov makes the poetic,
or the playful, speculation that Russian children
before the Revolution—and his exile—were
blessed with a surfeit of sensual impressions to
compensate them for what was to come. Of course,
fate doesn't play such premonitory games, but
memory can perform retrospective maneuvers to
compensate for fate. Loss is a magical preservative.

FROM *Lost in Translation: A Life in a New Language* (1989)

"**Therefore the** Lord God sent him forth from the garden of Eden, to till the ground from whence he was taken. So he drove out the man; and he placed at the east of the garden of Eden Cherubims, and a flaming sword which turned every way, to keep the way of the tree of life." Thus Genesis, on humankind's first exiles. Since then, is there anyone who does not—in some way, on some level—feel that they are in exile? We feel ejected from our first homes and landscapes, from childhood, from our first family romance, from our authentic self. We feel there is an ideal sense of belonging, of community, of attunement with others and at-homeness with ourselves, that keeps eluding us. The tree of life is barred to us by a flaming sword, turning this way and that to confound us and make the task of approaching it harder.

On one level, exile is a universal experience. But, of course, exile also refers to a specific social and political condition—although even in that sense, it was never a unitary category, and we tend to compress too many situations under its heading. The different circumstances surrounding individual migration, and the wider political or cultural contexts within which it takes place, can have enormous practical and psychic repercussions, reflected in the various words we use for those who leave one country for another. There are refugees, émigrés, emigrants, and expatriates, designations that point to distinct kinds of social, but also internal, experience. It matters enormously, for starters, whether you choose to leave or are forced to; it matters also whether you're coming to a new land unprotected and unprovided for or whether you can expect, or transport, some kind of safety net. When my family came from Poland to Canada, we were immigrants, a term that has connotations of class—lower than émigrés, higher perhaps than refugees—and degree of choice—more than is given to refugees, less than to expatriates.

Historically, too, the symbolic meaning and therefore the experience of exile has changed. In medieval Europe, exile was the worst punishment that could be inflicted. This was because one's identity was defined by one's role and place in society; to lose that was to lose a large portion of one's self. After being banished from Florence, Dante lived less than a hundred miles from his city-state—and yet he felt that his expulsion was a kind of psychic and social death, and his dream was either of return or of revenge (which he certainly executed very effectively in the *Inferno*). Real life, for Dante, was in Florence; it could not exist fully anywhere else. Joseph Conrad's father wrote to his infant son, who had been born during a time when Poland was erased from the map, "Tell yourself that you are without land, without love, without Fatherland, without humanity—as long as Poland, our Mother, is enslaved." In other words, for a patriot of an occupied nation, it was possible to feel radically exiled within that country, as long as it did not possess the crucial aspect of national sovereignty.

All of these forms of exile implied a highly charged concept of home—although that home was not necessarily coeval with one's birthplace. For the medieval clerics and church functionaries who traveled from monastery to monastery, the center of gravity was the city that housed the papal seat. The Jews have had the most prolonged historical experience of collective exile; but they survived their Diaspora—in the sense of preserving and maintaining their identity—by nurturing a powerful idea of home. That home existed on two levels: there were the real communities that Jews inhabited in various countries; but on the symbolic and perhaps the more important plane, home consisted of the entity "Israel," which increasingly became less a geographic and more a spiritual territory, with Jerusalem at its heart. While living in dispersion, Jews oriented themselves toward this imaginative center of the world, from which they derived their essential identity.

In our own century, the two great totalitarianisms, Nazi and Soviet, produced the most potent forms of exile, although the Soviet expulsions proved more permanent. The refugees from Nazi Germany, with their bright galaxy of artists and intellectuals—Hannah Arendt, Bertolt Brecht, Theodor Adorno, Herbert Marcuse, and others—were pushed from their country by a vile regime, but once the war was over, they could go back, and some chose to do so. The exiles from Eastern Europe—Vladimir Nabokov, Czeslaw Milosz, Milan Kundera, Joseph Brodsky, and others— thought that their banishment was for life, though history reversed it for some of them in the end.

But in recent years, in Europe most markedly, great tectonic shifts in the political and social landscape have taken place, which I think are affecting the very notion of exile—and of home. For what is happening today is that cross-cultural movement has become the norm rather than the exception, which in turn means that leaving one's native country is simply not as dramatic or traumatic as it used to be. The ease of travel and communication, combined with the loosening of borders following the changes of 1989, give rise to endless crisscrossing streams of wanderers and guest workers, nomadic adventurers and international drifters. Many are driven by harsh circumstance, but the element of voluntarism, of choice, is there for most. The people who leave the former Soviet Union nowadays are likely to be economic migrants or mafia tax dodgers buying up elegant real estate in London rather than dissidents expelled by ruthless state power. In one Bengali village, for example, there is a tradition of long seasonal migration, or sojourning. Many of the village's men leave for several years or even decades, but always with the intention of returning. These are hardly privileged émigrés or expatriates, but neither are they powerless victims of globalization. Instead, they are people with agency and intentionality, playing the system. Smart young men choose different countries for the timely economic advantages they offer—better wages, better interest rates. Almost all go back, a bit richer and a bit more important in the eyes of their fellow villagers. Theirs are migrations divested of tragedy if not of adversity.

Of course, there are still parts of the world, South America or Southeast Asia, where political dissidents are expelled by demagogic dictatorships and cannot return while those dictatorships endure. There are still refugees from Bosnia whose return is barred by the sword of violence. I do not mean to underestimate for a moment their hardships, but I would think that even in their case, the vastly increased mobility and communicative possibilities of our world change the premises of their banishment: friends can visit or phone; they know that if the government of their country changes—and political arrangements, along with everything else, have become susceptible to quicker change—they can go back, or travel back and forth.

The *Herald Tribune* recently characterized the increasing numbers of American expatriates in Europe: "They are the Americans abroad, and their number is soaring in a time when travel is unblinkingly routine, communications easy and instant, and telecommuting a serious option. They are abroad in a world where they can watch the Super Bowl live from a Moscow sports bar or send an e-mail from an Internet cafe in Prague."

Well, exactly. We all recognize these basic features of our new, fast-changing social landscape. Whether we have left or not, we know how easy it is to leave. We know that we live in a global village, although the village is very virtual indeed—a village dependent not on locality or the soil but on what some theorists call deterritorialization—that is, the detachment of knowledge, action, information, and identity from specific place or physical source. We have become less space-bound, if not yet free of time.

Simultaneously there has grown up a vast body of commentary and theory that is rethinking and revising the concept of exile and the related contrapuntal concept of home. The basic revision has been to attach a positive sign to exile and the cluster of mental and emotional experiences associated with it. Exile used to be thought of as a difficult condition. It involves dislocation, disorientation, self-division. But today, at least within the framework of postmodern theory, we have come to value exactly those qualities of experience that exile demands—uncertainty, displacement, the fragmented identity. Within this conceptual framework, exile becomes, well, sexy, glamorous, interesting. Nomadism and diasporism have become fashionable terms in intellectual discourse. What is at stake is not

only, or not even primarily, actual exile but our pre-
ferred psychic positioning, so to speak, how we situate
ourselves in the world. And these days we think the
exilic position has precisely the virtues of instability,
marginality, absence, and outsiderness. This privileging of exile compresses two things: first, a real descrip-
tion of our world, which indeed has become more
decentered, fragmented, and unstable, and second,
an approbation of these qualities, which is more prob-
lematic, because it underestimates the sheer human
cost of actual exile as well as some of its psychic impli-
cations, and perhaps even lessons.

My emigration took place during the Cold War,
though not in the worst Stalinist years. My parents
chose to leave, though that choice was so overdeter-
mined that it could hardly have been called "free."
But I happened to be a young and unwilling emigrant, yanked from my childhood, which I had
believed to be happy. Therefore, I felt the loss of my
first homeland acutely, fueled by the sense (the certain knowledge, it seemed then) that this departure
was irrevocable. Poland was abruptly sundered from
me by an unbridgeable gap; it was suddenly elsewhere, unreachable, on the other side, and I felt,
indeed, as if I were being taken out of life itself.

This kind of abrupt rupture breeds its own set of
symptoms and syndromes. It is, first of all, a powerful
narrative shaper; it creates chiaroscuro contrasts,
a stark sense of biographical drama. The stories
that emerged from the Cold War are legion, but one

certain outcome of exile that takes place in a bipolar world is the creation of a bipolar personal world. Spatially, the world becomes riven into two parts, divided by an uncrossable barrier. Temporally, the past is all of a sudden on one side of a divide, the present on the other.

Flash-forward to 1994, and a rather ordinary trip I took to Kraków that year with an English friend. The Westernization of my native town was everywhere evident. Where previously there had been no market, there was now commerce. Where before there was the great Eastern European nada, now there were boutiques, Krups coffee machines, Armani suits. It was perhaps the presence of my Western friend, who kept saying that Kraków looked like any small European city with a well-preserved historical center, that made me realize palpably what I had known in principle: that the differences between East and West were blurring pretty completely and that simultaneously the various divisions and oppositions I had set up in my inner landscape were shifting and blurring, too. When I came upon a lone shopwindow featuring a display familiar from the days of yore—a dry loaf of bread, an apple, and a desultory can of Coke—I pointed it out to my friend excitedly. Look! This was how it used to be! But this was not the way things were now. The dusty little vitrine was a trace, a remaining mark of a world that, for all its misery, had the appeal of familiarity and, most saliently, of clarity. Now I would have to live in a world in which the bipolar structure was gone, in which everything is intermingled and no site is more privileged—either in its deprivation or in its pleasures—than anywhere else. I would have to change my narrative.

At this vanishing of contrasts I confess that I felt not only relief but regret. It was a regret, undoubtedly perverse, for the waning of clarity. But I also felt the loss of the very sense of loss I had experienced on my emigration. For the paroxysm I experienced on leaving Poland was, for all the pain, an index of the significance I attached to what I left behind.

Still, what had I mourned in 1959? What was it that stood for home? Though I was too young to know it, the fervor of my feelings was produced by the Cold War. And yet my response had nothing of geopolitics about it. As a bare adolescent, I was too politically innocent to be a budding nationalist; in any case, as a daughter of Jewish parents recently transplanted from the Ukraine and not fully engaged in the body politic, I was in a poor position to become a patriot. So it was not the nation I felt exiled from, not Conrad's father's Poland; my homeland was made of something much earlier, more primary than ideology. Landscapes, certainly, and cityscapes, a sense of place. I was lucky enough to grow up in a city that really is quite enchanting and that escaped the ravages of the war. There was the webwork of friendships and other relationships, for example with my teachers. But there were also elements less palpable that nevertheless constituted my psychic home.

For the great first lessons of my uprooting were in the enormous importance of language and of culture. My first recognition, as I was prized out of familiar speech and social environment, was that these entities are not luxuries or even external necessities but the medium in which we live, the stuff of which we are made. In other words, they constitute us in a way of which we perhaps remain unconscious if we stay safely ensconced within one culture.

For a while, like so many emigrants, I was in effect without language, and from the bleakness of that condition, I understood how much our inner existence, our sense of self, depends on having a living speech within us. To lose an internal language is to subside into an inarticulate darkness in which we become alien to ourselves; to lose the ability to describe the world is to render that world a bit less vivid, a bit less lucid. And yet the richness of articulation gives the hues of subtlety and nuance to our perceptions and thought. To me, one of the most moving passages in Nabokov's writing is his invocation of Russian at the end of *Lolita.* There he summons not only the melodiousness or euphony of Russian sounds, compelling though these may be, but the depth and wholeness with which the original language exists within us. It is that relationship to language, rather than any more superficial mastery, that is so difficult to duplicate in languages one learns subsequently.

In more religious times, certain languages were considered sacred; that is, they were thought, in the words of a wonderful social historian, Benedict Anderson, to have "ontological reality inseparable from a single system of representation." Arabic, for example, was considered to be the only language in which the Koran could be written; the sacred texts could not be translated into any other language. So with Latin for the medieval Catholic church and Hebrew for Orthodox Jews. Some premodern people today still have the sense that their language is the true language, that it corresponds to reality in a way other languages don't. And it may be that one's first language has, for the child, this aura of sacrality. Because we learn it unconsciously, at the same time as we are learning the world, the words in one's first language seem to be equivalent to the things they name. They seem to express us and the world directly. When we learn a language in adulthood, we know that the words in it "stand for" the things they describe; that the signs on the page are only signs—arbitrary, replaceable by others. It takes time before a new language begins to inhabit us deeply, to enter the fabric of the psyche and express who we are.

As with language, so with culture: what the period of first, radical dislocation brought home was how much we are creatures of culture, how much we are constructed and shaped by it—and how much incoherence we risk if we fall out of its matrix. We know that cultures differ in customs, food, religions, social arrangements. What takes longer to understand is that each culture has subliminal values, predispositions, and beliefs that inform our most intimate assumptions and perceptions, our sense of beauty, for example, or of acceptable distances between people or notions of pleasure and pain. On that fundamental level, a culture does not exist independently of us but within us. It is inscribed in the psyche, and it gives form and focus to our mental and emotional lives. We could hardly acquire a human identity outside it, just as we could hardly think or perceive outside language. In a way, we are nothing more—or less—than an encoded memory of our heritage.

It is because these things go so deep, because they are not only passed on to us but *are* us, that one's original home is a potent structure and force and that being uprooted from it is so painful. Real dislocation, the loss of all familiar external and internal parameters, is not glamorous, and it is not cool. It is a matter not of willful psychic positioning but of an upheaval in the deep material of the self.

Is it then all pain and no gain? Of course not.

Being deframed, so to speak, from everything familiar, makes for a certain fertile detachment and gives one new ways of observing and seeing. It brings you up against certain questions that otherwise could easily remain unasked and quiescent, and brings to the fore fundamental problems that might otherwise simmer inaudibly in the background. This perhaps is the great advantage, for a writer, of exile, the compensation for the loss and the formal bonus—that it gives you a perspective, a vantage point.

The distancing from the past, combined with the sense of loss and yearning, can be a wonderful stimulus to writing. Joyce Carol Oates, in a striking formulation, has written that "for most novelists, the art of writing might be defined as the use to which we put our homesickness. So powerful is the instinct to memorialize in prose—one's region, one's family, one's past—that many writers, shorn of such subjects, would be rendered paralyzed and mute." In exile, the impulse to memorialize is magnified, and much glorious literature has emerged from it. *Native Realm* by Milosz or Nabokov's *Speak, Memory,* some of Brodsky's essays in *Less Than One,* or even Kundera's much cooler take on transplantation in *The Book of Laughter and Forgetting*—these are works of lyrical commemoration informed by a tenderness for what is lost and by the need, even the obligation, to remember.

But the perspective one gains from dislocation is, of course, not only retrospective but prospective. Exile places one at an oblique angle to one's new world and makes every emigrant, willy-nilly, into an anthropologist and relativist; for to have a deep experience of two cultures is to know that no culture is absolute—it is to discover that even the most interstitial and seemingly natural aspects of our identities and social reality are constructed rather than given and that they could be arranged, shaped, articulated in quite another way.

For this reason, too, exile can be a great impetus to thought and to creativity, which is why so many artists have actively chosen it: James Joyce, with his motto of "Silence, exile, and cunning"; Samuel Beckett with his decision to write in French rather than English, precisely for the advantages of defamiliarization. And for the nonwriter, too, biculturalism can have its bracing pleasures—the relish of sharpened insight, the savviness of skepticism—which can become positively addictive.

But I have come to believe that these virtues have their serious defects, that in the long term, the addiction may be too seductive, that as a psychological choice, the exilic position may become not only too arduous but too easy. Perhaps the chief risk of privileging the exilic narrative is a psychic split—living in a story in which one's past becomes radically different from the present and in which the lost homeland becomes sequestered in the imagination as a mythic, static realm. That realm can be idealized or demonized, but the past can all too easily become not only "another country" but a space of projections and fantasies. Some people decide to abandon the past, never to look back. For others, the great lure is nostalgia—an excess of memory. One of the most extreme examples of "living in the past" I've come across is the history of Polish refugee camps in England, which had been set up during World War II for people who had come there with the Polish army. These camps remained until the late 1950s, their inhabitants existing in virtual isolation, many never learning English and always hoping that the magic moment of redemption—the moment of return—was around the corner. But the actual Poland was no longer the one they remembered; it had changed in ways they would surely have found unpalatable, or at least highly perplexing, had they actually been able to go back.

For Jews in their long Diaspora, the need to preserve the symbolic center in an indifferent world—to keep intact a vision of a lost paradise and a promised land—often led them to insulate themselves from their surroundings, to retreat to their community as a place of refuge and spiritual fortress. I have written a book about the history of a shtetl in Poland, a small town whose population was half-Jewish, half-Polish.[1] The shtetl, for Eastern European Jews, was home in its most secure—internally secure, that is—form. In these small, rural enclaves, everyone knew everyone else, and everyone followed the same rules of behavior and spiritual life. No one was allowed to fall out of the communal net; no one needed to suffer from the modern malaise of uncertainty and alienation. The shtetl was a highly resilient, highly organized microsociety, and for many of its members, its strict codes and protective arrangements provided the satisfactions of warmth, safety, and certainty. But for others, the regulation of everyday life became oppressive, the avoidance of the larger world stifling.

------

1. *Shtetl: The Life and Death of a Small Town and the World of Polish Jews* (Boston: Houghton Mifflin, 1998).

Even before World War II, the metaphoric walls of the shtetl were beginning to break down. Many of its inhabitants, for various reasons, chose to leave literally; others began to question the structures of belief, causing heated conflicts within the shtetl itself.

Of course, the insulation of the shtetl was not only self-inflicted. But my point is that exile, and the pain of radical change, do not necessarily lead to a more radical personality structure or greater openness to the world. On the contrary, upheaval and dislocation can sometimes produce some rather more conservative impulses of self-defense and self-preservation. My own tendency was certainly to nostalgia and idealization—perhaps because I was ejected before my loss of innocence, before I could develop more considered opinions and preferences or revise my feelings about the place I came from. And once you leave, such revisions become very difficult.

In the later phases, the potential rigidity of the exilic posture may inhere not so much in a fixation on the past as in habitual detachment from the present. Such detachment can of course be a psychic, or even moral, luxury—but it comes at a price. In his fascinating, provocative essay "Exile as a Neurotic Solution,"[2] A. B. Yehoshua, a leading Israeli writer, makes the startling observation that during the eighteen

---

2. In Étan Levine, ed., *Diaspora: Exile and the Contemporary Jewish Condition* (New York: Steimatzky/Shapolsky, 1986).

hundred years of the Diaspora, there were many intervals when Jews could have settled in Palestine easily, or more easily, than in the countries where they chose to live, but that in fact, Palestine was the one place they consistently avoided. It was as if, he suggests, they were afraid precisely of reaching their promised land and the responsibilities and conflicts involved in turning the mythical Israel into an actual, ordinary home. Life in Diaspora had its enormous difficulties; but it offered the benefit of turning conflict outward, against a hostile or uncomprehending world, and thus avoiding the internal conflicts within the Jewish polity—conflicts that have certainly become evident since the founding of Israel (as they are in any functioning society).

Whatever the historical accuracy of Yehoshua's thesis, it does remind us of certain hazardous syndromes of the exiled stance: that this posture, if maintained too long, allows people to conceive of themselves as perpetually Other, and therefore unimplicated in the mundane, compromised, conflict-ridden locality that they inhabit; it allows them to imagine the sources and causes of predicaments as located outside, in a hostile or oppressive environment, rather than within.

In our current, habitually diasporic, habitually nomadic world, the oppositional, bipolar model no longer holds. The goalposts have shifted—indeed, the whole playing field has changed—in ways that remain elusive and hard to define. When all borders are crossable and all boundaries permeable, it is harder to project conflict outward, to imagine an idyllic realm or a permanent enemy. This is initially confusing, but it is surely to the good. Indeed, the merits of the new situation are easily discernible. They are the benefits available to those American expatriates who can leave America without ever really leaving. We move not only between places but between cultures with more grace and ease. We are less shocked by the varied assumptions prevailing among different peoples, less prone to absolutist assertions of our rightness. We have become tangibly aware of the plurality of values that such liberal thinkers as Isaiah Berlin have tried to teach us. In the political sphere, the ease of movement across borders should surely work to counter dogmatic or fanatical nationalism, although given the rise of national conflicts, this result may not be self-evident. But for those who move freely among countries and cultures, it becomes difficult to maintain the notion of any one nation's superiority or special destiny. The literature of this new nomadism or diasporism, of which Salman Rushdie is perhaps the most prominent representative, is a transnational literature in which multiple cultural references collide and collude and in which their interplay is seen as exactly that—robust, vital play. This is a vision of exile, if it can still be called that, as comedy, rather than despair.

Is it then, in this blithe new world, all gain and no pain? I don't quite think so.

The new nomadism is different from other Dias-
poras. It exists in a decentered world, one in which
the wanderers no longer trace and retrace a given
territory or look to any one symbolic locus of meaning. If we take such radical decentering as a
metaphor for a way of being and of selfhood, if we
rewrite displacement as the favored position (which
it holds in postmodern theory), then the model is
not without its own, sometimes high, costs. In the
Bengali village people have a suggestive way of talking about this: they say that their land has lost some of
its strength because its inhabitants are dispersed—as
if the land draws power from the loyalty and attachment of the humans who live on it. But I wonder if, in
our world of easy come, easy go, of traveling light and
sliding among places and meanings without alighting
on any of them for long, we don't risk a dispersion
of internal focus and perhaps even of certain
strengths—strengths that come from the gathering
of experiences so that they add up to memories, from
the accumulation of understanding, from placing
ourselves squarely where we are and living in a framework shared with others. I wonder if, in trying to exist
in liminal spaces, or conceiving of experience as
movement between discrete dots on a horizontal
map, we don't risk what Kundera calls the "unbear-
able lightness of being," the illness that comes upon
people unanchored in any place or structure, the
Don Juans of experience who travel perpetually
to new moments and sensations and to whom no

internal site—of attachment, need, desire—is more important than any other.

In the "bipolar" mentality, the idea of home may become too dramatized or sentimentalized. In the "nomadic" configuration, exile loses its charge, since there is no place from which one can be expelled, no powerful notion of home. Indeed, these days we are wont to say not so much that all fiction is homesickness as that all homesickness is fiction—that home never was what it was cracked up to be, the haven of safety and affection we dream of and imagine. Instead, home is conceived of mostly as a conservative site of enclosure and closure, of narrow-mindedness, patriarchal attitudes, and dissemination of nationalism. And, indeed, the notion of "home" may have been, in recent times, peculiarly overcharged, as the concepts of "country" and "nation" have been superimposed on each other with a seeming inevitability. "France," for the French, is both la belle France and la patrie. Such overlapping is not a necessary one. We have seen, for example, in the unhappy case of the former Yugoslavia, that a geographic territory can abruptly change its national identity. But the nostalgia of exiles for their birthplace has undoubtedly often been augmented by this conjunction of geographic and patriotic longing.

The transports of patriotism, narrowness of provincial perspectives, and confinements of parochial traditions are not plausible solutions to the dilemmas of our time. And yet continual dislocation, or dispersion,

is both facile and, in the long run, arid. Can anything
be rescued from the notion of home, or at-homeness,
that is sufficient to our condition?

One of the most interesting and subtle medita-
tions on home I know of is found in V. S. Naipaul's
autobiographical novel *The Enigma of Arrival.* The
place at which he was trying to arrive was a small cottage attached to a large house on a historic estate in
England. For Naipaul, this entails multiple ironies;
he grew up in an Indian community in Trinidad and
understands all too well that his very presence on the
estate is the end result of long imperial relations. He
also knows that the cottage, the manor, the ancient
plain, correspond for him to some fantasy of England
that he developed precisely when growing up in
Trinidad and that included some dream of perma-
nence, dignity, beauty. It takes a while before Naipaul
squares these preconceptions with the realities of the
place where he lives—realities that include change,
modernization, conflict. Slowly he begins to see the
landscape before him through other eyes. He imag-
ines how the estate looks to the temporary workers,
to whom a cottage with a thatched roof is simply temporary shelter, not a home, "a place to which you
could transfer (or risk transferring) emotion or
hopes." He begins to imagine how the estate looks
and feels to its owner, who suffers from accidie, a
melancholic withdrawal from the world; Naipaul
interprets this malaise as a symptom of the landlord's
excessive at-homeness, a security that has become

a stasis. He understands that the power relations of today are complex enough to confer on him some advantages unavailable to his aristocratic landlord—the advantages of dynamism, of ambition, even of need. Slowly Naipaul learns to read the landscape in a less romantic and more complex way. He comes to love the place from the position not of fantasy but of knowledge.

The slowness of this process is crucial; in Naipaul's book, that ruminative leisureliness makes the act of creating a home akin to the process of writing. It is through gradual accretion of details, of knowledge, of relationships that he comes to imaginative possession of the place, as he comes to imaginative possession of his subject.

Naipaul's understated allegory suggests that there are two kinds of homes: the home of our childhood and origin, which is a given, a fate, for better or for worse, and the home of our adulthood, which is achieved only through an act of possession, hard-earned, patient, imbued with time, a possession made of our choice, agency, the labor of understanding, and gradual arrival.

The experience of enforced exile paradoxically accentuates the potency of what is given, of the forces that have shaped us before we could shape ourselves. This is what Brodsky says about the magnetic pull of one's parental home and the exile's dilemma of having wandered away—or having been forced to wander—too far:

For a while, he is absorbed with new vistas,
absorbed with building his own nest,
with manufacturing his own reality. Then
one day, when the new reality is mastered,
when his own terms are implemented,
he suddenly learns that his old nest is gone,
that those who gave him life are dead. On
that day he feels like an effect suddenly
without a cause. . . . What he can't blame on
nature is the discovery that his achievement,
the reality of his own manufacture, is less
valid than the reality of his abandoned nest.
That if there ever was any-thing real in his
life, it was precisely that nest, oppressive and
suffocating, from which he so badly wanted
to flee. He knows how willful, how intended
and premeditated everything that he has
manufactured is. How, in the end, all of it
is provisional.[3]

I agree and sympathize, even empathize, with this
almost entirely. The acute loss I felt on emigrating was
commensurate with the depth of my attachment—
and there is something about that that I don't want to
disavow, and which can be a source of later perceptions and affections. After leaving Russia, Nabokov

---

3. Joseph Brodsky, "A Room and a Half," in his *Less Than One: Selected Essays* (New York: Farrar, Straus & Giroux, 1986), end of section 18.

wrote in several languages masterfully, but he was transposing the love of his first language to his subsequent ones. We need to develop a model in which the force of our first legacy can be transposed or brought into dialogue with our later experiences, in which we can build new meanings as valid as the first ones. This can be done only through a deepening investigation, through familiarization. It is fine, and illuminating, to see all the structures that construct us for what they are and to see through them; but we must acknowledge the need for frameworks that contain us, for sites that are more than temporary shelters. And we need to see that in our world it may be insufficient to define ourselves as Other in opposition to some archetypal oppressor or hypothetical insider. Our societies are too fragmented to have an easily discernible inside or permanent centers of power. At the same time, we need a conception of a shared world, a world in which we exist by virtue of shared interests rather than mutual alienation, to which we can bring our chosen commitments and hopes.

There is a Hasidic parable about the Baal Shem Tov, the founder of the Hasidic movement. In the parable, thieves come to the Baal Shem Tov and tell him of a network of underground corridors and tunnels that leads directly from Poland to Palestine. They offer to take him there, and he agrees. They walk through the tunnels with great difficulty. At one point, they come to a murky bog, which almost stops them. But they persist. They get more than halfway to their destination. Then, suddenly, the Baal Shem Tov sees before him "a flaming sword, turning this way and that," and decides to go no farther. He turns back to the place from which he started.

The psychological or mythological meaning of this parable has had many interpretations. Perhaps on one level it says something about the Baal Shem Tov's ambivalence about going to Palestine, his own neurotic solution. But I think that the parable's unconscious, compressed message may be that you can't steal into paradise. You can't approach the tree of life by a shortcut. Of course, the parable also suggests something about the fearsomeness of approaching our object of desire and finding ourselves in paradise—which may then turn out to be an ordinary garden, needing weeding, tilling, and watering.

To be sure, in our human condition, it takes long, strenuous work to find the wished-for terrains of safety or significance or love. And it may often be easier to live in exile with a fantasy of paradise than to suffer the inevitable ambiguities and compromises of cultivating actual, earthly places. And yet, without some move of creating homing structures for ourselves, we risk a condition of exile that we do not even recognize as banishment. And paradoxically, if we do not acknowledge the possibility and the real pain of expulsion, then we will not know that somewhere there is a tree of life that, if we labor hard enough to approach it, can yield fruits of meaning after all.

Imagining Homelands

Bharati Mukherjee

My life, I now realize, falls into three disproportionate parts. Till the age of eight I lived in the typical joint family, indistinguishable from my twenty cousins, indistinguishable, in fact, from an eternity of Bengali Brahmin girls. From eight till twenty-one we lived as a single family, enjoying for a time wealth and confidence. And since twenty-one I have lived in the West. Each phase required a repudiation of all previous avatars; an almost total rebirth.

FROM *Days and Nights in Calcutta* (1977)

This essay is about four narratives, those of expatriation, exile, immigration, and repatriation. From those sub-narratives, I hope to weave a revisionist theory for contemporary residency and citizenship, or at least to suggest new terms in the unresolved debate that threatens to grow louder and more rancorous in years to come.

The question, as always, is, What is America? Is it a place or an idea, is it a patchwork of diverse communities, or a nuanced, accented, multicolored myth of shared values? Are we heading, in these final years of the millennium, toward the ancient dream of unity through diversity—*e pluribus unum*—or have we already taken the first steps down the long slope to chaos? Far from unity, we can't seem to find consensus on anything these days, not on affirmative action, on national educational standards, on needle exchanges, on family values, a drug policy, a trade policy, Most-Favored-Nation status for China, environmental protection, medical care, bilingual education, or even the designated hitter rule.

Both tendencies, chaos and unity, have attended our history. We are both a liberal experiment and a bulwark of reaction. De Tocqueville saw both tendencies, as did Lincoln, Faulkner, Melville and Emerson, and W.E.B. Du Bois, Frederick Douglass, and Martin Luther King, Jr.

I'm not a historian, only a fiction writer born and raised on a different continent who did not even become an American citizen until a dozen years ago. My work is set almost entirely within "immigrant communities," as they are so designated, although seen from the inside there is little that is communal about them, and only a minority of their inhabitants are even immigrants. Nevertheless, it is the reality of transplantation and psychological metamorphosis that is my material, not the world I left behind. I call myself an American writer, not an Indian one. I do not do this for material advantage (as Indian critics often assume), for there is far more commercial interest in the West in the India of tropical languor, dowry-death, and caste-strife than in scraped-knuckled, bruised-elbow immigration. I do it because I see in the process of immigration (in its widest sense, including at least three stages that have very little to do with changing citizenship) the stage, and the battleground, for the most exciting dramas of our time. A neighborhood like Jackson Heights, Queens, is on a par with Renaissance Venice for its richness of character and depth of intrigue. The same is true of my current home of San Francisco, my teaching campus of Berkeley, of Miami and Brooklyn, San Antonio and Detroit.

The national myth of immigration, the heart-warming saga of babushka-clad refugees climbing to the deck of the tramp steamer for a glimpse of the Statue of Liberty ("Look, Mama, just like the pictures we saw in Minsk, or Abruzzi, or Crete"), is just that, an image out of aging newspapers or our collective pop-memory banks. Today's arrivals are more likely to be discharged on a beach and told to swim ashore, or dropped in a desert and told to run, if they survive at all. Immigration, as I experience it, is made up of several conflicting parts. For my purposes here, "immigration" refers to the act of adopting new citizenship, of going the full nine yards of transformation. As such, it is but one option to be exercised by noncitizens living in this country.

Definitions seem to be in order. *Expatriation* is an act of sustained self-removal from one's native culture, balanced by a conscious resistance to total inclusion in the new host society. The motives for expatriation are as numerous as the expatriates themselves: aesthetic and intellectual affinity, a better job, a more interesting or less hassled life, greater freedom or simple tax relief, just as the motives for nonintegration may range from principle, to nostalgia, to laziness or fear. The roster of notable expatriates in the realm of literature alone is immensely long, rich in honors and deep in respect: Henry James, T. S. Eliot, Joseph Conrad, V. S. Naipaul (before their formal acceptance of British citizenship), Vladimir Nabokov, James Joyce, Samuel Beckett, Paul Bowles, Mavis Gallant, Gabriel García Márquez, Witold Gombrowicz, Anthony Burgess, Graham Greene, Derek Walcott, Malcolm Lowry, Wilson Harris—names, even with a few glaring omissions that any literate audience can fill in, that we'd all agree rise to the top of any listing of the twentieth century's most notable literary achievements.

They are, in fact, our great voices of modernism as well as a few of postmodernism; their works are encyclopedic, their visions ironic and penetrating, their analyses detached and scrupulous, their styles experimental yet crystalline. If the ultimate goal of literature is to achieve universality and a kind of god-like omniscience, expatriation—the escape from small-mindedness, from niggling irritations—might well be a contributing factor.

The expatriate is the ultimate self-made artist, even the chooser of a language in which to operate, as Conrad, Beckett, Kundera, and Nabokov testify, an almost literal exponent of Joyce's dream of self-forging in the smithy of his soul. It is possible, in expatriation, to step out of the constraints into which one has been born and to exercise to the fullest the dual vision of the detached outsider. The expatriate Hungarian, Czech, or Pole of an earlier era, or today's Yugoslav or Bangladeshi, Algerian or Palestinian expatriate, asks only that the host culture permit him or her to retain an alien core that will not be compromised or surrendered. The bargain is thus struck: I will be a model resident. In return for your tolerance and noninterference, I will not attack the fundamental flaws of your society with anything like the zeal I bring to the dissection of my own people. I will imagine a new homeland built on reclaimed land.

I confess it is an attractive bargain, one which I entertained myself, many years ago.

In the case of *exile*, the comparative luxury of self-removal is replaced by harsh compulsion. The spectrum of choice is gravely narrowed; the alternatives may be no more subtle than death, imprisonment, or a one-way ticket to oblivion. We all cheered the arrival of Aleksandr Solzhenitsyn in America, thinking we would gain a new voice in our literature as we did with Auden and Isherwood, or a new superstar as we have with so many singers and actors, or sensational tennis players. The list of twentieth-century exiles is an alternate Who's Who of Nobel listings in the sciences and literature, as well as an honor roll of world-class painters, dancers, performers, and composers. In some cases, the urgency of exile may, in time, blend into the serendipity of expatriation—Milan Kundera in Paris, Picasso in Arles, Chaplin in Switzerland—but for the most part, the exile does not achieve the same Olympian detachment enjoyed by the expatriate. The exile is still tied to a mother country and a major cause that are the source of his wounding, and he may or may not choose, or have the option of choosing, to translate his passions or his words. The United States at present is home to dozens of exiles writing in their native Spanish and Russian and Arabic, in Chinese and Burmese, in Tamil and Aramaic, publishing in their own form of *samizdat* or exile presses, interviewed on ethnic radio and reviewed in the ethnic press, and few of us will ever have the good fortune to read their work or know of

their existence. Similar, if not larger, populations cluster in Paris, Toronto, and London, in Berlin and Mexi-
co City, in Amsterdam and Barcelona.[1]
Exile lacks the grandeur, the majesty, of expatriation. The expatriate, at least, is validated by a host culture which extends the hospitality, and he often
returns it in civic dutifulness. But the exile is a peti-
tioner. He brings with him the guilty reminders of
suffering, his stay is provisional and easily revoked,

---

1. Exile may become the subject of great literature, but it does
not encourage the conditions for its production. For every
Solzhenitsyn or Thomas Mann, every Freud, Kundera, or
Skvorecky, every Ngugi wa Thiong'o or Wole Soyinka, every Liu
Binyan, there are still today's Isaac Babels trapped behind the
lines of their own despotisms. Read the heartbreaking reports of
Amnesty International or of PEN's Freedom to Write committee
and you will learn that the free world is still comparatively blind
and deaf to the fate of Algerian, Turkish, Iranian, Malaysian,
Indonesian, Cuban, Chinese, Burmese, Sierra Leonean, Niger-
ian, Egyptian, Cambodian, Tamil, and Sinhalese dissidents. Their
names are not known, their causes are not sexy, their languages
are not in wide distribution in the West, and for these reasons,
along with those of trade and political influence, their lives, their
bravery, and their work go unvalidated.
It makes you wonder, sometimes, if anyone stays at home. Is
some sort of major disruption essential for great writing? Of
course that's not the truth, as even a moment's reflection can
show, but the list of expatriate and exiled writers is nevertheless a
daunting one to contemplate. It might be truer to say that all writers are expatriates to one degree or another, or they are internal
exiles; certainly William Faulkner or Flannery O'Connor,
Bernard Malamud or Cynthia Ozick, hail from a country without
a passport.

and he is often consigned to the underworld of ethnic intrigue, outside the purview of the law or of the press. If expatriation is the route of cool detachment, exile is for some that of furious engagement.

I must confess my own years of furious engagement, not in this country, but in my husband's Canada. When we lived in the Greek neighborhoods of Montréal, we were brought into daily contact with the passions of pro- and anti-"Colonels" Greek immigrants, the threats of arson by pro-junta Greeks on anti-junta businesses. In Toronto and Vancouver, the early years of the Punjab civil war were playing themselves out on the streets of various Little Indias. In all cases, police response, despite appeals for protection by what are called in Canada "visible minorities," and by simple Canadian citizens such as myself, harassed on the streets and in public transportation by white youths, was a variant of "It's not our [meaning white, Canadian] problem. You guys"—or more likely, *you little people*—"settle it among yourselves."[2]

In November 1996, *The New York Times* asked me to contribute an op-ed piece inspired by the so-called

---

2. I should add that it very much was a "white, Canadian" problem. The eventual outcome of such racist smugness was the bloodiest terrorist act of modern times, the blowing up, by a small group of Sikh extremists, of an Air-India 747 over the coast of Ireland, with the loss of 329 Canadian lives. If you can find a copy of the book, The Sorrow and the Terror, which my husband and I co-authored in 1987, you'll understand some of the urgency that has motivated both of our writings since that tragic event.

immigration debate that was then raging on both sides during the election battle. Are we "all immigrants," as the pietistic national myth would have it, therefore duty-bound to support immigration as an apple pie or motherhood issue, or are most new immigrants cheats and rip-off artists, as many nativists seem to believe?

I chose to write of my older sister and myself, two Calcutta-born women from identical backgrounds with the same Cambridge-tested accent, the same convent education, who have been in the United States for over thirty-five years. My sister married an Indian student in Detroit and has remained in the same job and the same house, wearing saris, cooking familiar food, guarding the accent, for the past thirty years. She holds the much-valued U.S. green card but feels her home is still India, where she intends to retire in the next few years. I, too, married a fellow student in the Writers' Workshop at the University of Iowa, an American of Canadian parentage, and we have lived in Canada and in several parts of the United States, moving at least twenty times, and have often been obliged by professional circumstances to live many years apart. I am a U.S. citizen and could not imagine returning to India for other than family visits and relaxed vacations. My accent is an amalgam of the places I've lived, my wardrobe is a similar hodgepodge, and so is our daily menu.

The question I meant to raise was simply this: which one of us is the freak? Someone who retains the food, the clothes, the accent of expatriation, or her T-shirted, blue-jeaned sister? The answer is by no means clear. That little article, anecdotal in nature, aroused more passions than many of my novels. When I give readings or interviews in India, it becomes a lead-question (the article was reprinted in several Indian newspapers), and the questioners are often anything but cordial. Conversely, the article has been celebrated by the liberal mainstream in this country as a bold statement of faith in the American experiment, warts and all. Neither reaction is entirely satisfactory.

Among some Indian intellectuals it is read as a polarizing document, an implicit rejection of the worth of hundreds of thousands of law-abiding, tax-paying, communally and religiously conservative, contributing Indian nationals, like my sister, working and residing overseas. At its fringes, that interpretation tends to bracket my pro-immigration, let-it-go stance with those of some unsavory company, English-only, "America First"-ers of a stripe with Enoch Powell or the current crop of French and Austrian race-baiters who even propose cleansing the various European motherlands of Turks, Gypsies, North Africans, Kurds, and Bosnian/Kosovo refugees. We all know the end-point of such appeals to purity, especially in Europe.

Given my presumed respectability in the United States as a member of a prominent minority community, and my access to mainstream media, I try at every

opportunity to distinguish my position from those of
ill-disposed, anti-immigrant Americans as well as
of instinctive Americaphobes, a large number of
whom, unfortunately, can be found among India-born
academics in American universities. I know I'm not the
only person from a minority community who weighs
American promise against American history on a daily
basis and who still finds a positive balance, but it still
seems necessary to emphasize my basic position. I am
an integrationist and, to use a deliberately ugly word, a
mongrelizer. My sister, like most expatriates or exiles,
is not. Mongrels lose a lot of prestige and pedigree in
their travels, they're not as classically proportioned or
predictably behaved as purebreds, and, more to the
point, their presence creates a third, unpredictable,
sometimes undesirable and often untrainable mutt.
Because I am here, I am changed totally by you and by
my commitment to this country and its problems, but
so are you. You are now implicated in my life, you probably entrust your health, or aspects of it, to Indian doctors or dentists, you can now eat my food in nearly any
town, run India-designed software on your India-
designed computer. I'm just as mainstream as anyone
else. I am also a proud India-born, Bengali-speaking
Hindu. These positions need not be antithetical.

Like my academic colleagues with whom I have
conducted many public quarrels, I too grew up in a
British-centered universe in India. As a college student I too would have snickered at the pretense of an
American culture, of an American literature. To

declare my Americanness, and not to retain the genteel expatriation of an upper-class Bengali Brahmin, is, in their minds, to be linked with and to share the historical guilt of slavery, segregation, extermination of Native Americans, the CIA, Vietnam, and to be linked with the hypocrisy of supporting both freedom and dictatorships, and with a generally vulgar "Coca-Cola" and "McDonald's" culture.

That is a far less comforting heritage than that of my forebears, at least as it was communicated to me. My city, my religion, my caste, were always the innocent victims of foreign invaders. We were the colonized, the humiliated, the despised. History had cleansed us of all ancestral sins. Many of my colleagues apparently still believe in the myth of national innocence, and will do anything to maintain it.

The tale of two sisters of course suggests larger narratives, those of expatriation and those of immigration. The narrative of expatriation calls to mind villas in the south of France, on the shores of Lake Geneva, apartments in Paris, but it is no stranger to Detroit as well. The narrative of expatriation fairly drips with respectability, or at least with privilege, but the narrative of immigration calls to mind crowded tenements, Ellis Island, sweatshops, accents, strange foods, taxicab drivers, bizarre holidays, strange religions, unseemly ethnic passions.

And it must be admitted, especially in New York City, that the narrative of immigration is a scripted cliché. Little Italy, the Lower East Side, Chinatown,

Brighton Beach, Yorkville, Harlem, the South Bronx, the Upper East Side, the Upper West Side—we can almost populate those neighborhoods from central casting, from war movies, B-movies, TV drama, sitcoms, and musicals. It is a cliché because it is the story of the parents and grandparents of second- and third-generation Americans and it's been handed over to *me* and to millions like me, unchanged. The narrative turned out happily, in general; the poor became middle class, the foreign became more American than Americans, traditional national values were not deeply challenged, but were even upheld and strengthened. (For those who didn't fit in, and there were many, things turned out differently. Sacco and Vanzetti were executed, so was Bruno Hauptmann, so were the Rosenbergs.) It's a cliché because the language has not been updated.

Central-casting immigration is European, white, Christian and Jewish. The distance between America and Europe a hundred years ago seemed vast, unimaginable; the linguistic, cultural, and religious differences tested the very limits of contemporary assimilation. Of course, more alien populations were simply barred from any thought of immigration. Asians were "sojourners" whose wives were not admitted; African Americans were denied the vote; Latinos and French-Canadians (who were called "blue-eyed Chinese") clustered in enclaves near their borders; they were considered unassimilable.

The immigration narrative changed with the end of colonialism. Vast populations were no longer hemmed in by colonial legislation. The old European-favored quota system was challenged; talent, merit, and family unification became an aim of immigration policy. The new arrivals were no longer populating an empty landscape or providing muscle for labor-intensive heavy industry.

We Americans fought bitter wars in alien areas, we disrupted civilizations and admitted some of the survivors. The Cold War sent its refugees to Florida, to Brooklyn, to Minneapolis. We wanted professionals, we needed doctors, engineers, researchers, and entrepreneurs. We educated the Third World's brightest in our schools and then we kept them. They brought in their parents, their cousins, they sponsored others. Immigrant communities grew from a dozen epicenters, from Queens to Glendale, Miami to Minnesota, and each community became self-sustaining. Dithering and cynical politics allowed uncountable millions of undocumented workers to enter, and while their net value to the economy is not really in dispute, their likely contribution to a broadening of American democracy certainly is, especially if they are kept underground, not permitted to educate their children or to enjoy some semblance of public acceptance. In California, we can already see how we've permitted the situation to coarsen the public dialogue.

There are now Little Indias, Koreas, Jamaicas, Colombias, Saigons, Moscows, Mexicos, Vientianes, Manilas, Chinas, in cities that had never experienced immigration communities in earlier waves. My concern is definitely not with their presence here, it is with our ability *to adjust to* their presence and to make it a productive, that is, a mongrelizing encounter. If five million undocumented aliens are now in the country, living in slums and barrios, working at odd jobs, hiding from authorities, sending money home, neglecting their children, engaging in criminal activity (my New York apartment was ransacked by that most innocent icon of Manhattan life, the Chinese take-out delivery man, whose hotbox contained an acetylene torch for cutting through my firedoor), we may never encounter one another except in figurative dark alleys—and that is an immigration tragedy.

Immigration may be an uplifting narrative, but it's not pretty and certainly not elegant, like expatriation. It's low-tech. I am an immigrant, and to achieve that honor, I gave up status that I'll never be able to achieve in the New World. I became this thing new to U.S. history, someone who had never existed before me and hundreds of thousands like me: an Indo-American. As a writer, I had to decide how to describe myself—Asian-American, Indo-American, unhyphenated American? I claim myself as an American in the immigrant tradition of writers I most admire, Henry Roth and Bernard Malamud; yet it is still, after fifteen years of aggressive correction, a rare literary notice that does not identify me as "Indian." It's apparently easier for Monica Seles to be accepted as American than me, and I wonder why that might be.

We are still fighting the tradition of nineteenth-century exclusivism, the branding of the "visibly foreign" or the non-Judeo/Christian as unsuited for naturalization. It was the price paid by native-born Japanese-Americans in World War II, by the Latino-appearing in Los Angeles, by Asians just about anywhere: accepted as "sojourners" doing dirty and underpaid work, but not as Americans altering the appearance, eventually, of us all.

There is a fourth narrative, not often mentioned, but one which complicates even the murkier aspects of immigration. I think of it as repatriation, a repopulation of formerly Spanish lands, formerly French lands, formerly Native American lands, which involves the undocumented movement of millions over borders that we may think of as unviolable but which others have long considered mere extensions of their homeland. When my husband, Clark Blaise, was researching a book about his French-Canadian father, he was struck by the fact that Léo Blais's native village in Québec was part of the same parish that reached into Maine, that family members were buried on both sides of the border, that my father-in-law could emigrate from Canada in 1912 and arrive in Manchester, New Hampshire, work in the mills and go to school and never learn a word of English. What was true in New England ninety years ago has always been true in the Rio Grande Valley and East Los Angeles; it has become the rule in South Florida, in East Harlem and the South Bronx. If we speak seriously of the Pacific Rim, and of profiting from its markets and asserting our influence upon it, we are implicitly inviting all Asia to our shores—particularly if our history also includes a significant amount of historical "collateral damage," as in the case of the Philippines and Vietnam. It's America's own version of Israel's Law of Return. Immigrant groups are reclaiming their lands and feel no need to make apologies or accommodations to the latest landlords. Geography is once again dictating destiny. (Anyone who doubts it should take a look at Vancouver, British Columbia, now a virtual extension of Hong Kong.) We English-speakers are a minority in the New World, we are integrating our economies, and the implication is that we must adjust to the free movement of workers in much the way Europe does today.

Expatriation, exile, immigration, and repatriation, four ways of accommodating the modern restlessness, the modern dislocations, the abuses of history, the hopes of affluence. It seems to me we have entered a supra-national age, in which traditional citizenship is likely to be a murky identification, and where technical proficiency is the true passport to acceptance. Somehow, we must find a way of integrating all four modes of entry into our narrative of Americanism, for the cruelties of history itself have imposed too heavy a burden on the normal channels of transformation.

With the pietistic formula "we are all immigrants," I have to disagree. We are not, and never were. We have reinvented the myths of our founding so many

times, and for so many audiences, that we've probably lost all trace of a unifying narrative. Many never
had the chance to immigrate; many never wanted to.
Did we come seeking religious freedom? I didn't. Did
we come to escape oppression, the shackles of dicta-
torship? I didn't. Did we rejoin the remnants of our
scattered family? I didn't. Have we come seeking happiness and fortune?—for both, I should have stayed
where I was. We are expatriates, exiles, slaves, and dis-
possessed, we are conquerers, plunderers, refugees,
and amnesty-seekers, we are temporary workers,
undocumented workers, visitors, students, tourists,
we are joy-seekers, claim-jumpers, parole-violators.

While it would not work for me, and I do feel the
process of classic immigration has liberated me in
ways that expatriation never could, I must be prepared to accept the validity of my sister Mira's narrative of expatriation and those of others like her. Their
voices are hidden inside me, I have written some of
their stories, and I grieve for them far more than I
resent them—it's a reaction curiously similar to that
of most Third World writers toward the work of V. S.
Naipaul. "Damn him," I want to shout, damn his supe-
rior airs, damn his cold detachment, damn his vast talent, damn his crystalline sentences. I want him to
manifest love, for just a paragraph or two, to cut loose.
This does not affect my respect for his work. I want my
sister to feel love for this country that she, in the
depths of her heart, cannot. This does not affect the
contribution she makes to schoolchildren in Detroit.

I have met the undocumented and I have written about them; I too want them to know some of our freedoms, I want them to know relief from poverty, from fear of deportation, from exploitation, but I realize America will never be more for them than a chance to work, to pocket a little money and snatch a little fun. It was their country and we were the interlopers, and in their hearts and in their history it is still their land. For us to call them aliens in those strings of mission-named California cities, we must surrender a bit of our own sanity.

We must be prepared to accept the bitter, exiled discourse, whether it comes from the Cuban-Americans of Miami, the Vietnamese of California, or the Russian Jews of Brighton Beach and Los Angeles, their tight defensiveness, their aggressiveness, their blinkered vision. And what of the vast minority discourse in this country, the African American expressions with their anti-Semitic and anti-Asian notes, their own internal dispute with the world that brought them here, that refused to integrate them but then stole every degree of their self-expression?

And beyond that, we must understand, and truly accept, that the United States for all its power is only a minority state. It must accommodate itself to the preponderance of Latin Americans on this hemisphere, and it must understand that part of its core is the acceptance of the cruel fact of its minority status.

No Reconciliation Allowed

Edward W. Said

Exile is predicated on the existence of, love for,
and a real bond with one's native place; the universal
truth of exile is not that one has lost that love or
home, but that inherent in each is an unexpected,
unwelcome loss. Regard experiences then as if
they were about to disappear: what is it about them
that anchors or roots them in reality? What would
you save of them, what would you give up, what
would you recover?

FROM *Culture and Imperialism* (1993)

ᘝ

In the first book I wrote, *Joseph Conrad and the Fiction of Autobiography*, published more than thirty years ago, and then in an essay called "Reflections on Exile" that appeared in 1984, I used Conrad as an example of someone whose life and work seemed to typify the fate of the wanderer who becomes an accomplished writer in an acquired language, but can never shake off his sense of alienation from his new—that is, acquired— and, in Conrad's rather special case, admired home.[1] His friends all said of Conrad that he was very contented with the idea of being English, even though he never lost his heavy Polish accent and his quite peculiar moodiness, which was thought to be very un-English. Yet the moment one enters his writing, the aura of dislocation, instability, and strangeness is unmistakable. No one could represent the fate of lostness and disorientation better than he did, and no one was more ironic about the effort of trying to replace that condition

------

1. *Joseph Conrad and the Fiction of Autobiography* (Cambridge, Mass.: Harvard University Press, 1966); and "Reflections on Exile," *Granta* 13 (Autumn 1984): 159–72.

with new arrangements and accommodations—which invariably lured one into further traps, such as those Lord Jim encounters when he starts life again on his little island. Marlow enters the heart of darkness to discover that Kurtz was not only there before him but is also incapable of telling him the whole truth; so that, in narrating his own experiences, Marlow cannot be as exact as he would have liked, and ends up producing approximations and even falsehoods of which both he and his listeners seem quite aware.

Only well after his death did Conrad's critics try to reconstruct what has been called his Polish background, very little of which had found its way directly into his fiction. But the rather elusive meaning of his writing is not so easily supplied, for even if we find out a lot about his Polish experiences, friends, and relatives, that information will not of itself settle the core of restlessness and unease that his work relentlessly circles. Eventually we realize that the work is actually constituted by the experience of exile or alienation, which cannot ever be rectified. No matter how perfectly he is able to express something, the result always seems to him an approximation of what he had wanted to say, and to have been said too late, past the point where the saying of it might have been helpful. "Amy Foster," the most desolate of his stories, is about a young man from Eastern Europe, shipwrecked off the English coast on his way to America, who ends up as the husband of the affectionate but inarticulate Amy Foster. The man remains a foreigner, never learns the language, and even after he and Amy have a child cannot become a part of the very family he has created with her. When he is near death and babbling deliriously in a strange language, Amy snatches their child from him, abandoning him to his final sorrow. Like so many of Conrad's fictions, the story is narrated by a sympathetic figure, a doctor who is acquainted with the pair, but even he cannot redeem the young man's isolation, although Conrad teasingly makes the reader feel that he might have been able to. It is difficult to read "Amy Foster" without thinking that Conrad must have feared dying a similar death, inconsolable, alone, talking away in a language no one could understand.

The first thing to acknowledge is the loss of home and language in the new setting, a loss that Conrad has the severity to portray as irredeemable, relentlessly anguished, raw, untreatable, always acute—which is why I have found myself over the years reading and writing about Conrad like a *cantus firmus*, a steady groundbass to much that I have experienced. For years I seemed to be going over the same kind of thing in the work I did, but always through the writings of other people. It wasn't until the early fall of 1991 when an ugly medical diagnosis suddenly revealed to me the mortality I should have known about before that I found myself trying to make sense of my own life as its end seemed alarmingly nearer. A few months later, still trying to assimilate my new condition, I found myself composing a long explanatory letter to my mother, who had already been dead for almost two years, a letter that inaugurated a belated attempt to impose a narrative on a life that I had left more or less to itself, disorganized, scattered, uncentered. I had had a decent enough career in the university, I had written a fair amount, I had acquired an unenviable reputation (as the "professor of terror") for my writing and speaking and being active on Palestinian and generally Middle Eastern or Islamic and anti-imperialist issues, but I had rarely paused to put the whole jumble together. I was a compulsive worker, I disliked and hardly ever took vacations, and I did what I did without worrying too much (if at all) about such matters as writer's block, depression, or running dry.

All of a sudden, then, I found myself brought up short with some though not a great deal of time available to survey a life whose eccentricities I had accepted like so many facts of nature. Once again I recognized that Conrad had been there before me—except that Conrad was a European who left his native Poland and became an Englishman, so the move for him was more or less within the same world. I was born in Jerusalem and had spent most of my formative years there and, after 1948, when my entire family became refugees, in Egypt. All my early education had, however, been in elite colonial schools, English public schools designed by the British to bring up a generation of Arabs with natural ties to Britain. The last one I went to before I left the Middle East to go to the United States was Victoria College in Cairo, a school in effect created to educate those ruling-class Arabs and Levantines who were going to take over after the British left. My contemporaries and classmates included King Hussein of Jordan, several Jordanian, Egyptian, Syrian, and Saudi boys who were to become ministers, prime ministers, and leading businessmen, as well as such glamorous figures as Michel Shalhoub, head prefect of the school and chief tormentor when I was a relatively junior boy, whom everyone has seen on screen as Omar Sharif.

The moment one became a student at Victoria College one was given the school handbook, a series of regulations governing every aspect of school life—the kind of uniform we were to wear, what equipment was needed for sports, the dates of school holidays, bus schedules, and so on. But the school's first rule, emblazoned on the opening page of the handbook, read: "English is the language of the school; students caught speaking any other language will be punished." Yet there were no native English-speakers among the students. Whereas the masters were all British, we were a motley crew of Arabs of various kinds, Armenians, Greeks, Italians, Jews, and Turks, each of whom had a native language that the school had explicitly outlawed. Yet all, or nearly all, of us spoke Arabic—many spoke Arabic and French—and so we were able to take refuge in a common language in defiance of what we perceived as an unjust colonial stricture. British imperial power was nearing its end immediately after World War II, and this fact was not lost on us, although I cannot recall any student of my generation who would have been able to put anything as definite as that into words.

For me, there was an added complication, in that although both my parents were Palestinian—my mother from Nazareth, my father from Jerusalem—my father had acquired U.S. citizenship during World War I, when he served in the AEF under Pershing in France. He had originally left Palestine, then an Ottoman province, in 1911, at the age of sixteen, to escape being drafted to fight in Bulgaria. Instead, he went to the United States, studied and worked there for a few years, then returned to Palestine in 1919 to go into business with his cousin. Besides, with an unexceptionally Arab family name like Said connected to an improbably British first name (my mother very much admired the Prince of Wales in 1935, the year of my birth), I was an uncomfortably anomalous student all through my early years: a Palestinian going to school in Egypt, with an English first name, an American passport, and no certain identity at all. To make matters worse, Arabic, my native language, and English, my school language, were inextricably mixed: I have never known which was my first language, and have felt fully at home in neither, although I dream in both. Every time I speak an English sentence, I find myself echoing it in Arabic, and vice versa.

All this went through my head in those months after my diagnosis revealed to me the necessity of thinking about final things. But I did so in what for me was a characteristic way. As the author of a book called *Beginnings*,[2] I found myself drawn to my early days as a boy in

---

2. *Beginnings: Intention and Method* (New York: Basic Books, 1975).

Jerusalem, Cairo, and Dhour el Shweir, the Lebanese
mountain village which I loathed but where for years
and years my father took us to spend our summers. I
found myself reliving the narrative quandaries of my
early years, my sense of doubt and of being out of place,
of always feeling myself standing on the wrong corner,
in a place that seemed to be slipping away from me just
as I tried to define or describe it. Why, I remember asking myself, could I not have had a simple background,
been all Egyptian, or all something else, and not have
had to face the daily rigors of questions that led back to
words that seemed to lack a stable origin? The worst
part of my situation, which time has only exacerbated,
has been the warring relationship between English and
Arabic, something that Conrad had not had to deal
with since his passage from Polish to English via French
was effected entirely within Europe. My whole education was Anglocentric, so much so that I knew a great
deal more about British and even Indian history and
geography (required subjects) than I did about the history and geography of the Arab world. But although
taught to believe and think like an English schoolboy, I
was also trained to understand that I was an alien, a
Non-European Other, educated by my betters to know
my station and not to aspire to being British. The line
separating Us from Them was linguistic, cultural,
racial, and ethnic. It did not make matters easier for me
to have been born, baptized, and confirmed in the
Anglican Church, where the singing of bellicose hymns
like "Onward Christian Soldiers" and "From Green-

land's Icy Mountains" had me in effect playing the role
at once of aggressor and aggressed against. To be at the
same time a Wog and an Anglican was to be in a state of
standing civil war.

In the spring of 1951 I was expelled from Victoria
College, thrown out for being a troublemaker, which
meant that I was more visible and more easily caught
than the other boys in the daily skirmishes between
Mr. Griffith, Mr. Hill, Mr. Lowe, Mr. Brown, Mr. Maun-
drell, Mr. Gatley, and all the other British teachers, on
the one hand, and us, the boys of the school, on the
other. We were all subliminally aware, too, that the old
Arab order was crumbling: Palestine had fallen, Egypt
was tottering under the massive corruption of King
Farouk and his court (the revolution that brought
Gamal Abdel Nasser and his Free Officers to power
was to occur in July 1952), Syria was undergoing a
dizzying series of military coups, Iran, whose Shah was
at the time married to Farouk's sister, had its first big
crisis in 1951, and so on. The prospects for deracinat-
ed people like us were so uncertain that my father
decided it would be best to send me as far away as possible—in effect, to an austere, puritanical school in
the northwestern corner of Massachusetts.

The day in early September 1951 when my mother
and father deposited me at the gates of that school and
then immediately left for the Middle East was probably
the most miserable of my life. Not only was the atmos-
phere of the school rigid and explicitly moralistic, but
I seemed to be the only boy there who was not a native-

born American, who did not speak with the required
accent, and who had not grown up with baseball, bas-
ketball, and football. For the first time ever, I was
deprived of the linguistic environment I had depend-
ed on as an alternative to the hostile attentions of
Anglo-Saxons whose language was not mine, and who
made no bones about my belonging to an inferior, or
somehow disapproved, race. Anyone who has lived
through the quotidian obstacles of colonial routine
will know what I am talking about. One of the first
things I did was to look up a teacher of Egyptian origin
whose name had been given to me by a family friend in
Cairo. "Talk to Ned," our friend said, "and he'll
instantly make you feel at home." On a bright Saturday
afternoon I trudged over to Ned's house, introduced
myself to the wiry, dark man who was also the tennis
coach, and told him that Freddie Maalouf in Cairo had
asked me to look him up. "Oh yes," the tennis coach
said rather frostily, "Freddie." I immediately switched
to Arabic, but Ned put up his hand to interrupt me.
"No, brother, no Arabic here. I left all that behind
when I came to America." And that was the end of that.

Because I had been well trained at Victoria College,
I did well enough in my Massachusetts boarding
school, achieving the rank of either first or second in a
class of about a hundred and sixty. But I was also found
to be morally wanting, as if there was something myste-
riously not-quite-right about me. When I graduated,
for instance, the rank of valedictorian or salutatorian
was withheld from me on the grounds that I was not fit

for the honor—a moral judgment which I have ever
since found difficult either to understand or to for-
give. Although I went back to the Middle East on vacations (my family continued to live there, moving from
Egypt to Lebanon in 1963), I found myself becoming
an entirely Western person; both at college and in
graduate school I studied literature, music, and philos-
ophy, but none of it had anything to do with my own
tradition. During the 1950s and early 60s, students
from the Arab world were almost invariably scientists,
doctors, and engineers, or specialists in the Middle
East, getting degrees at places like Princeton and Harvard and then, for the most part, returning to their
countries to become teachers in universities there. I
had very little to do with them, for one reason or
another, and this naturally increased my isolation from
my own language and background. By the time I came
to New York to teach at Columbia in the fall of 1963, I
was considered to have an exotic, but somewhat irrele-
vant Arabic background—in fact I recall that it was easier for most of my friends and colleagues not to use the
word "Arab," and certainly not "Palestinian," prefer-
ring the much easier and vaguer "Middle Eastern," a
term that offended no one. A friend who was already
teaching at Columbia later told me that when I was
hired I had been described to the department as an
Alexandrian Jew! I remember a sense of being accepted, even courted, by older colleagues at Columbia,
who with one or two exceptions saw me as a promising,
even very promising, young scholar of "our" culture.

Since there was no political activity then that was centered on the Arab world, I found that my concerns in my teaching and research, which were canonical though slightly unorthodox, kept me within the pale.

The big change came with the Arab-Israeli war of 1967, which coincided with a period of intense political activism on campus over civil rights and the Vietnam war. I found myself naturally involved on both fronts, but, for me, there was the further difficulty of trying to draw attention to the Palestinian cause. After the Arab defeat there was a vigorous reemergence of Palestinian nationalism, embodied in the resistance movement located mainly in Jordan and the newly occupied territories. Several friends and members of my family had joined the movement, and when I visited Jordan in 1968, 69, and 70, I found myself among a number of like-minded contemporaries. In the United States, however, my politics were rejected—with a few notable exceptions—both by anti-war activists and by supporters of Martin Luther King, Jr. For the first time I felt genuinely divided between the newly assertive pressures of my background and language and the complicated demands of a situation in the United States that scanted, in fact despised, what I had to say about the quest for Palestinian justice—which was considered anti-Semitic and Nazi-like.

In 1972 I had a sabbatical and took the opportunity to spend a year in Beirut, where most of my time was taken up with the study of Arabic philology and literature, something I had never done before, at least not at that level, out of a feeling that I had allowed the disparity between my acquired identity and the culture into which I was born, and from which I had been removed, to become too great. In other words, there was an existential as well as a felt political need to bring one self into harmony with the other, for as the debate about what had once been called "the Middle East" metamorphosed into a debate between Israelis and Palestinians, I was drawn in, ironically enough, as much because of my capacity to speak as an American academic and intellectual as by the accident of my birth. By the mid-70s I was in the rich but unenviable position of speaking for two diametrically opposed constituencies, one Western, the other Arab.

For as long as I can remember, I had allowed myself to stand outside the umbrella that shielded or accommodated my contemporaries. Whether this was because I was genuinely different, objectively an outsider, or because I was temperamentally a loner I cannot say, but the fact is that although I went along with all sorts of institutional routines because I felt I had to, something private in me resisted them. I don't know what it was that caused me to hold back, but even when I was most miserably solitary or out of synch with everyone else, I held onto this private aloofness very fiercely. I may have envied friends whose language was one or the other, or who had lived in the same place all their lives, or who had done well in accepted ways, or who truly belonged, but I do not recall ever thinking that any of that was possible for me. It wasn't that I considered myself special, but rather that I didn't fit the situations I found myself in and wasn't too displeased to accept this state of affairs. I have, besides, always been drawn to stubborn autodidacts, to various sorts of intellectual misfit. In part it was the heedlessness of their own peculiar angle of vision that attracted me to writers and artists like Conrad, Vico, Adorno, Swift, Adonis, Hopkins, Auerbach, Glenn Gould, whose style, or way of thinking, was highly individualistic and impossible to imitate, for whom the medium of expression, whether music or words, was eccentrically charged, very worked-over, self-conscious in the highest degree. What impressed me about them was not the mere fact of their self-invention but that the enterprise was deliberately and fastidiously located within a general history which they had excavated *ab origine*.

Having allowed myself gradually to assume the professional voice of an American academic as a way of submerging my difficult and unassimilable past, I began to think and write contrapuntally, using the disparate halves of my experience, as an Arab and as an American, to work with and also against each other. This tendency began to take shape after 1967, and though it was difficult, it was also exciting. What prompted the initial change in my sense of self, and in the language I was using, was the realization that in accommodating to the exigencies of life in the U.S. melting pot, I had willy-nilly to accept the principle of annulment of which Adorno speaks so perceptively in *Minima Moralia*:

The past life of émigrés is, as we know,
annulled. Earlier it was the warrant of arrest,
today it is intellectual experience, that is
declared non-transferable and unnaturaliz-
able. Anything that is not reified, cannot
be counted and measured, ceases to exist.
Not satisfied with this, however, reification
spreads to its own opposite, the life that
cannot be directly actualized; anything that
lives on merely as thought and recollection.
For this a special rubric has been invented.
It is called "background" and appears on
the questionnaire as an appendix, after sex,
age and profession. To complete its viola-
tion, life is dragged along on the triumphal
automobile of the united statisticians, and
even the past is no longer safe from the
present, whose remembrance of it consigns
it a second time to oblivion.[3]

For my family and for myself, the catastrophe of
1948 (I was then twelve) was lived unpolitically. For
twenty years after their dispossession and expulsion
from their homes and territory, most Palestinians had
to live as refugees, coming to terms not with their past,
which was lost, annulled, but with their present. I do

3. Theodor Adorno, *Minima Moralia: Reflections from Damaged Life,* trans. by E.F.N. Jephcott (London: New Left Books, 1974), pp. 46–47.

not want to suggest that my life as a schoolboy, learning
to speak and coin a language that let me live as a citizen
of the United States, entailed anything like the suffering of that first generation of Palestinian refugees, scattered throughout the Arab world, where invidious laws
made it impossible for them to become naturalized,
unable to work, unable to travel, obliged to register and
reregister each month with the police, many of them
forced to live in appalling camps like Beirut's Sabra and
Shatila, which were the sites of massacres thirty-four
years later. What I experienced, however, was the
suppression of a history as everyone around me celebrated Israel's victory, its terrible swift sword, as Barbara
Tuchman grandly put it, at the expense of the original
inhabitants of Palestine, who now found themselves
forced over and over again to prove that they had once
existed. "There are no Palestinians," said Golda Meir in
1969, and that set me, and many others, the slightly
preposterous challenge of disproving her, of beginning
to articulate a history of loss and dispossession that had
to be extricated, minute by minute, word by word, inch
by inch, from the very real history of Israel's establish-
ment, existence, and achievements. I was working in an
almost entirely negative element, the non-existence,
the non-history which I had somehow to make visible
despite occlusions, misrepresentations, and denials.

Inevitably, this led me to reconsider the notions of
writing and language, which I had until then treated as
animated by a given text or subject—the history of the
novel, for instance, or the idea of narrative as a theme

in prose fiction. What concerned me now was how a subject was constituted, how a language could be formed—writing as a construction of realities that served one or another purpose instrumentally. This was the world of power and representations, a world that came into being as a series of decisions made by writers, politicians, philosophers to suggest or adumbrate one reality and at the same time efface others. The first attempt I made at this kind of work was a short essay I wrote in 1968 entitled "The Arab Portrayed,"[4] in which I described the image of the Arab that had been manipulated in journalism and some scholarly writing in such a way as to evade any discussion of history and experience as I and many other Arabs had lived them. I also wrote a longish study of Arabic prose fiction after 1948 in which I reported on the fragmentary, embattled quality of the narrative line.

During the 1970s I taught my courses in European and American literature at Columbia and elsewhere, and bit by bit entered the political and discursive worlds of Middle Eastern and international politics. It is worth mentioning here that for the forty years that I have been teaching I have never taught anything other than the Western canon, and certainly nothing about the Middle East. I've long had the ambition of giving a course on modern Arabic literature, but I haven't

4. "The Arab Portrayed," pp. 1–9 in Ibrahim Abu-Lughod, ed., *The Arab-Israeli Confrontation of June 1967: An Arab Perspective* (Evanston, Ill.: Northwestern University Press, 1970).

gotten around to it, and for at least thirty years I've
been planning a seminar on Vico and Ibn Khaldun, the
great fourteenth-century historiographer and philoso-
pher of history. But my sense of identity as a teacher of
Western literature has excluded this other aspect of my
activity so far as the classroom is concerned. Ironically,
the fact that I continued to write and teach my subject
gave sponsors and hosts at university functions at which
I had been invited to lecture an excuse to ignore my
embarrassing political activity by specifically asking me
to lecture on a literary topic. And there were those who
spoke of my efforts on behalf of "my people," without
ever mentioning the name of that people. "Palestine"
was still a word to be avoided.

Even in the Arab world Palestine earned me a great
deal of opprobrium. When the Jewish Defense League
called me a Nazi in 1985, my office at the university was
set fire to and my family and I received innumerable
death threats, but when Anwar Sadat and Yasser Arafat
appointed me Palestinian representative to the peace
talks (without ever consulting me) and I found it impossible to step outside my apartment, so great was the
media rush around me, I became the object of extreme
left-wing nationalist hostility because I was considered
too liberal on the question of Palestine and the idea of
coexistence between Israeli Jews and Palestinian Arabs.
I've been consistent in my belief that no military option
exists for either side, that only a process of peaceful reconciliation, and justice for what the Palestinians have
had to endure by way of dispossession and military occu-

pation, would work. I was also very critical of the use of slogan-clichés like "armed struggle" and of the revolutionary adventurism that caused innocent deaths and did nothing to advance the Palestinian case politically. "The predicament of private life today is shown by its arena," Adorno wrote. "Dwelling, in the proper sense, is now impossible. The traditional residences we grew up in have grown intolerable: each trait of comfort in them is paid for with a betrayal of knowledge, each vestige of shelter with the musty pact of family interests." Even more unyieldingly, he continued:

> The house is past. . . . The best mode of
> conduct, in the face of all this, still seems
> an uncommitted, suspended one: to lead
> a private life, as far as the social order and
> one's own needs will tolerate nothing else,
> but not to attach weight to it as something
> still socially substantial and individually
> appropriate. "It is even part of my good
> fortune not to be a house-owner," Nietzsche
> already wrote in *The Gay Science*. Today we
> should have to add: it is part of morality not
> to be at home in one's home.[5]

For myself, I have been unable to live an uncommitted or suspended life: I have not hesitated to declare

---

5. Adorno, pp. 38–39.

my affiliation with an extremely unpopular cause. On the other hand, I have always reserved the right to be critical, even when criticism conflicted with solidarity or with what others expected in the name of national loyalty. There is a definite, almost palpable discomfort to such a position, especially given the irreconcilability of the two constituencies, and the two lives they have required.

The net result in terms of my writing has been to attempt a greater transparency, to free myself from academic jargon, and not to hide behind euphemism and circumlocution where difficult issues have been concerned. I have given the name "worldliness" to this voice, by which I do not mean the jaded savoir-faire of the man about town, but rather a knowing and unafraid attitude toward exploring the world we live in. Cognate words, derived from Vico and Auerbach, have been "secular" and "secularism" as applied to "earthly" matters; in these words, which derive from the Italian materialist tradition that runs from Lucretius through to Gramsci and Lampedusa, I have found an important corrective to the German Idealist tradition of synthesizing the antithetical, as we find it in Hegel, Marx, Lukács, and Habermas. For not only did "earthly" connote this historical world made by men and women rather than by God or "the nation's genius," as Herder termed it, but it suggested a territorial grounding for my argument and language, which proceeded from an attempt to understand the imaginative geographies fashioned and then imposed by power on distant lands and people. In *Orientalism* and *Culture and Imperialism*,[6] and then again in the five or six explicitly political books concerning Palestine and the Islamic world that I wrote around the same time, I felt that I had been fashioning a self who revealed for a Western audience things that had so far either been hidden or not discussed at all. Thus, in talking about the Orient, hitherto believed to be a simple fact of nature, I tried to uncover the long-standing, very varied geographical obsession with a distant, often inaccessible world that helped Europe to define itself by being its opposite. Similarly, I believed that Palestine, a territory effaced in the process of building another society, could be restored as an act of political resistance to injustice and oblivion.

Occasionally, I'd notice that I had become a peculiar creature to many people, and even a few friends, who had assumed that being Palestinian was the equivalent of being something mythological like a unicorn or a hopelessly odd variation of a human being. A Boston psychologist who specialized in conflict resolution, and whom I had met at several seminars involving Palestinians and Israelis, once rang me from Greenwich Village and asked if she could come uptown to pay me a visit. When she arrived, she walked in, looked incredulously at my piano—"Ah, you actually play the piano," she said, with a trace of disbelief in her voice—and then

---

6. *Orientalism* (New York: Pantheon Books, 1978; reissued, with new Afterword, New York: Vintage Books, 1994); and *Culture and Imperialism* (New York: Knopf, 1993).

turned around and began to walk out. When I asked her whether she would have a cup of tea before leaving (after all, I said, you have come a long way for such a short visit), she said she didn't have time. "I only came to see how you lived," she said without a hint of irony. Another time, a publisher in another city refused to sign my contract until I had lunch with him. When I asked his assistant what was so important about having a meal with me, I was told that the great man wanted to see how I handled myself at the table. Fortunately, none of these experiences affected or detained me for very long: I was always in too much of a rush to meet a class or a deadline, and I quite deliberately avoided the self-questioning that would have landed me in a terminal depression. In any case, the Palestinian intifada that erupted in December 1987 confirmed our people-hood in as dramatic and compelling a way as anything I might have said. Before long, however, I found myself becoming a token figure, hauled in for a few hundred written words or a ten-second soundbite testifying to "what the Palestinians are saying," and I determined to escape that role, especially given my disagreements with the PLO leadership from the late 1980s on.

I am not sure whether to call this a kind of perpetual self-invention or a constant restlessness. Either way, I've long since learned to cherish it. Identity as such is about as boring a subject as one can imagine. Nothing seems less interesting than the narcissistic self-study that today passes in many places for identity politics, or ethnic studies, or affirmations of roots, cultural pride, drum-beat-

ing nationalism, and so on. We have to defend peoples
and identities threatened with extinction or subordinat-
ed because they are considered inferior, but that is very
different from aggrandizing a past invented for present
reasons. Those of us who are American intellectuals owe
it to our country to fight the coarse anti-intellectualism,
bullying, injustice, and provincialism that disfigure its
career as the last superpower. It is far more challenging
to try to transform oneself into something different
than it is to keep insisting on the virtues of being American in the ideological sense. Having myself lost a country with no immediate hope of regaining it, I don't find
much comfort in cultivating a new garden, or looking
for some other association to join. I learned from
Adorno that reconciliation under duress is both cow-
ardly and inauthentic: better a lost cause than a tri-
umphant one, more satisfying a sense of the provisional
and contingent—a rented house, for example—than
the proprietary solidity of permanent ownership. This is
why strolling dandies like Oscar Wilde or Baudelaire
seem to me intrinsically more interesting than extollers
of settled virtue like Wordsworth or Carlyle.

For the past five years I have been writing two
columns a month for the Arabic press; and despite my
extremely anti-religious politics, I am often glowingly
described in the Islamic world as a defender of Islam,
and considered by some of the Islamic parties to be one
of their supporters. Nothing could be further from the
truth, any more than it is true that I have been an apol-
ogist for terrorism. The prismatic quality of one's writ-

ing when one isn't entirely of any camp, or a total partisan of any cause, is difficult to handle, but there, too, I have accepted the irreconcilability of the various conflicting, or at least incompletely harmonized, aspects of what, cumulatively, I appear to have stood for. A phrase by Günter Grass describes the predicament well: that of the "intellectual without mandate." A complicated situation arose in late 1993 when, after seeming to be the approved voice of the Palestinian struggle, I wrote increasingly sharply of my disagreements with Arafat and his bunch. I was immediately branded "anti-peace" because I had the lack of tact to describe the Oslo treaty as deeply flawed. Now that everything has ground to a halt, I am regularly asked what it is like to be proved right, but I was more surprised by that than anyone: prophecy is not part of my arsenal.

For the past three or four years, I have also been trying to write a memoir of my early—that is, pre-political—life, largely because I think it's a story worthy of rescue and commemoration, given that the three places I grew up in have ceased to exist. Palestine is now Israel, Lebanon, after twenty years of civil war, is hardly the stiflingly boring place it was when we spent our summers locked up in Dhour el Shweir, and colonial, monarchical Egypt disappeared in 1952. My memories of those days and places remain extremely vivid, full of little details that I seem to have preserved as if between the covers of a book, full also of unexpressed feelings generated out of situations and events that occurred decades ago but seem to have been waiting to be articulated now.

Conrad says in *Nostromo* that a desire lurks in every heart to write down once and for all a true account of what happened, and this certainly is what moved me to write my memoir, just as I had found myself writing a letter to my dead mother out of a desire once again to communicate something terribly important to a primordial presence in my life. "In his text," Adorno says,

> the writer sets up house. . . . For a man
> who no longer has a homeland, writing
> becomes a place to live. . . . [Yet] the
> demand that one harden oneself against
> self-pity implies the technical necessity
> to counter any slackening of intellectual
> tension with the utmost alertness, and
> to eliminate anything that has begun to
> encrust the work or to drift along idly,
> which may at an earlier stage have served,
> as gossip, to generate the warm atmosphere
> conducive to growth, but is now left behind,
> flat and stale. In the end, the writer is not
> even allowed to live in his writing.[7]

One achieves at most a provisional satisfaction, which is quickly ambushed by doubt, and a need to rewrite and redo that renders the text uninhabitable. Better that, however, than the sleep of self-satisfaction and the finality of death.

------

7. Adorno, p. 87.

Refugees

Charles Simic

"Cameo Appearance"

I had a small nonspeaking part
In a bloody epic. I was one of the
Bombed and fleeing humanity.
In the distance our great leader
Crowed like a rooster from a balcony.
Or was it a great actor
Impersonating our great leader?

That's me there, I said to the kiddies.
I'm squeezed between the man
With two bandaged hands raised
And the old woman with her mouth open
As if she were showing us a tooth

That hurts badly. The hundred times
I rewound the tape, not once
Could they catch sight of me
In that huge gray crowd,
That was like any other gray crowd.

Trot off to bed, I said finally.
I know I was there. One take
Is all they had time for.
We ran, and the planes grazed our hair.
And then they were no more
As we stood dazed in the burning city.
But, of course, they didn't film that.

FROM *Walking the Black Cat* (1996)

Mine is an old, familiar story by now. So many people have been displaced in this century, their numbers so large, their collective and individual destinies so varied, it's impossible for me or anyone else, if we are honest, to claim any special status as a victim. Particularly since what happened to me fifty years ago is happening to someone else today. Rwanda, Bosnia, Afghanistan, Congo, the endlessly humiliated Kurds—and so it goes. Fifty years ago it was fascism and communism, now it's nationalism and religious fundamentalism that make life miserable in lots of places. Recently, for instance, I was translating the work of a woman poet from Sarajevo for an anthology, and its editors had great difficulty locating her. She had vanished. She was not a young woman, she had plenty of friends, but no one seemed to know what had happened to her in the confusion of the war. It took many months to find her sweeping floors in a restaurant in Germany.

"Displaced persons" is the name they had for us back in 1945, and that's what we truly were. As you sit watching bombs falling in some old documentary, or the armies advancing against each other, villages and

towns going up in fire and smoke, you forget about
the people huddled in the cellar. Mr. and Mrs. Innocent and their families paid dearly in this century for
just being there. Condemned by history, as Marxists
were fond of saying, perhaps belonging to a wrong
class, wrong ethnic group, wrong religion—what
have you—they were and continue to be an unpleasant reminder of all the philosophical and nationalist
utopias gone wrong. With their rags and bundles and
their general air of misery and despair, they came in
droves from the East, fleeing evil with no idea where
they were running to. No one had much to eat in
Europe and here were the starving refugees, hundreds of thousands of them in trains, camps, and pris-
ons, dipping stale bread into watery soup, searching
for lice on their children's heads and squawking in
dozens of languages about their awful fate.

My family, like so many others, got to see the world
for free thanks to Hitler's wars and Stalin's takeover
of Eastern Europe. We were not German collabora-
tors or members of the aristocracy, nor were we,
strictly speaking, political exiles. Small fry, we made
no decisions ourselves. It was all arranged for us by
the world leaders of the times. Like so many others
who were displaced, we had no ambition to stray far
beyond our neighborhood in Belgrade. We liked it
fine. Deals were made about spheres of influence,
borders were redrawn, the so-called Iron Curtain was
lowered, and we were set adrift with our few posses-
sions. Historians are still documenting all the treach-

eries and horrors that came our way as the result of
Yalta and other such conferences, and the subject is
far from finished.

As always, there were degrees of evil and degrees
of tragedy. My family didn't fare as badly as others.
Thousands of Russians whom the Germans forcibly
brought to work in their factories and on their farms
were returned to Stalin against their will by the Allies.
Some were shot and the rest packed off to the gulags
so they would not contaminate the rest of the citizen-
ry with newly acquired decadent capitalist notions.
Our own prospects were rosier. We had hopes of end-
ing up in the United States, Canada, or Australia. Not
that this was guaranteed. Getting into the United
States was especially difficult. Most Eastern European
countries had very small quotas, unlike the Western
European ones. In the eyes of the American genetic
experts and immigration policymakers, South Slavs
were not highly desirable ethnic material.

It's hard for people who have never experienced it
to truly grasp what it means to lack proper documents. We read every day about our own immigration
officers, using and misusing their recently acquired
authority to turn back suspicious aliens from our borders. The pleasure of humiliating the powerless must
not be underestimated. Even as a young boy, I could
see that was the case. Everywhere there are bureau-
crats, the police state is an ideal.

I remember standing in endless lines in Paris at
police headquarters to receive or renew resident per-

mits. It seems like that's all we ever did when we lived there. We'd wait all day only to discover that the rules had changed since the last time, that they now required, for instance, something as absurd as my mother's parents' marriage certificate or her grade-school diploma, even though she was in possession of a French diploma since she did her post-graduate studies in Paris. As we'd stand there pondering the impossibility of what they were asking of us, we'd be listening to someone at the next window trying to convey in poor French how the family's house had burned, how they'd left in a hurry with only one small suitcase, and so on, to which the official would shrug his shoulders and proceed to inform them that unless the documents were produced promptly, the residence permit would be denied.

So what did we do? Well, if the weather was nice we'd go and sit outside on a bench and watch the lucky Parisians stroll by carrying groceries, pushing baby carriages, walking their dogs, even whistling. Occasionally a couple would stop in front of us to smooch while we cursed the French and our rotten luck. In the end, we'd trudge back to our small hotel room and write home.

The mail didn't travel very swiftly, of course. We would go nuts every day for weeks waiting for the mailman, who couldn't stand the sight of us since we were always pestering him, and finally, somehow, the documents would arrive thanks to a distant relative. Then they had to be translated by an official transla-

tor who, of course, couldn't make heads or tails out of
the dog-eared fifty-year-old entry in a provincial
Balkan school or church registry. In any case, eventually we'd go back to the long line only to discover that
they were not needed after all, but something else
was. Every passport office, every police station, every
consulate had a desk with a wary and bad-tempered
official who suspected us of not being what we
claimed to be. No one likes refugees. The ambiguous
status of being called a DP made it even worse. The
officials we met knew next to nothing about where we
came from and why, but that did not prevent them
from passing judgment on us. Having been driven out
by the Nazis brought us a measure of sympathy, but
having left because of the Communists was not as well
received. If the officials were leftists, they told us
bluntly that, ungrateful wretches that we were, we had
left behind the most progressive, the most just society
on the face of the earth. The others figured we were
just riffraff with fake diplomas and a shady past. Even
the smiling dummies in store windows on the elegant
Avenue Victor Hugo regarded us as if we were out to
steal something. It was actually all extremely simple:
either we were going to get a foothold here or somewhere else, or we were going back to a refugee camp,
prison, or, even worse, to "the embodiment of man's
dearest longing for justice and happiness," as the
communist world was described in certain quarters.

Immigration, exile, being uprooted and made a
pariah may be the most effective way yet devised

to impress on an individual the arbitrary nature of his or her own existence. Who needed a shrink or a guru when everyone we met asked us who we were the moment we opened our mouths and they heard the accent?

The truth is, we had no simple answers. Being rattled around in freight trains, open trucks, and ratty ocean-liners, we ended up being a puzzle even to ourselves. At first, that was hard to take; then we got used to the idea. We began to savor it, to enjoy it. Being nobody struck me personally as being far more interesting than being somebody. The streets were full of these "somebodys" putting on confident airs. Half the time I envied them; half the time I looked down on them with pity. I knew something they didn't, something hard to come by unless history gives you a good kick in the ass: how superfluous and insignificant in any grand scheme mere individuals are. And how pitiless are those who have no understanding that this could be their fate too.

I stepped off the boat in New York City on August 10, 1954, with my mother and my brother. The day was hot, the sky was cloudless, and the streets were full of people and cars. My father, who was already in the United States, put us up in a hotel just off Times Square. It was incredible, astonishing. The immigration officers didn't torment us and rip up our papers.

They didn't send us back. Our being here and breath-
ing was perfectly legal. Watching TV, ordering room
service, and taking a shower broke no laws. Every half
hour, we asked my father again if this was true. When
he told us yes, we literally jumped for joy. No New
Year's Eve, no birthday celebration, no party afterward
ever gave me as much happiness. A fear had lifted.

"My love of the country follows from my love of its
freedoms," Lewis Lapham said, and I know that's
true. I felt that the first day I came to America and I
still feel the same.

I was sixteen, old enough to take walks by myself.
The city, which I had seen in so many movies, felt
strangely familiar. I'm a big city boy and all large cities
resemble one another in a fundamental way. Walking
around confirms what one already knows. Here's
where the rich live, here the poor. Here is where business is conducted and the expensive stores are to be
found. And finally, here is the neighborhood where
one goes to have a good time. Nobody had to explain
to me the difference between the young women I saw
on Madison Avenue and the ones hanging around a
candy store on Eighth Avenue. It was the same in Paris
and in Belgrade. Of course, New York is also unlike
any European city. Its bright colors were startling after
the grayness of Europe. Guys in pink shirts, wearing
neckties with palm trees on them, getting into yellow
taxis on a street of huge neon signs and billboards
showing smiling, rosy-cheeked faces drinking tea and
puffing cigarettes. That was really something.

Architecturally, too, the city was full of surprises. A skyscraper in midtown next to a three-story building with a hot dog stand. Water towers, fire escapes, trash on the sidewalks, a street with a dozen movie houses all showing films twenty-four hours a day and then a building seemingly made entirely of glass and a park with carriages pulled by horses. The question a new-comer asks, inevitably, is, Where am I going to live? Is it going to be a tenement in Hell's Kitchen or one of the brownstones on some quiet side street on the Upper East Side?

Our initial needs and worries were few and basic. First, and most importantly, we wanted new clothes and an American haircut to take away that look of a hopeless loser that comes with being a DP. We spent the first few days in New York changing our disguises. Jeans, Hawaiian shirts, cowboy belts, colorful T-shirts, sneakers, and other such items, procured cheaply in the vicinity of Times Square, appeared to me to be the height of elegance. To my great surprise, the natives still gave me funny looks on the street. Unwit-tingly I had transformed myself from a European schoolboy to a country hick, the kind you often saw around the Port Authority Bus Terminal or outside a 42nd Street movie house showing westerns.

Then there was the problem of language. I had studied English, could read it more or less, but speak-ing it was a different matter. I remember asking for directions the second or third day in New York and not being understood. I wanted to know how many blocks to the Empire State Building. A simple question, except that instead of "blocks," I said "corners." The astonishment and the embarrassment of speaking and not being able to communicate are deeply humbling. Every day in America, I realized, I would have a fresh opportunity to make a complete fool of myself. Quickly, I learned to keep my mouth shut except when absolutely necessary. In the meantime, I read the movie marquees, I tried to follow the TV and radio programs. In secrecy I repeated words and phrases I overheard: Hey, smart aleck! Crackerjack. Okeydokey. Chase butterflies. Hogwash. Hold the phone. Go to the dogs.

Then there was food. All these burgers, cherry Cokes, hot dogs, grilled cheese sandwiches, apple pies à la mode, and dozens of different candy bars had to be sampled. If you've grown up on thick soups and casseroles, American fast food has the advantage of being portable. It's hard to eat spaghetti or goulash in bed or in a car; it's much easier with a bag of chips or a can of peanuts. It's a perfect invention for someone hungry all the time, as I was. It sounds nice intellectually to claim that an expatriate can never feel at home anywhere again. It's definitely not true of a sixteen year old. I was more adaptable than a cat or a goldfish would have been. I was eager to see and taste everything.

Once, my father's rich boss invited us to his house for a Sunday meal. We expected a huge feast and were astonished by the canned vegetables and the thin, overcooked slices of roast beef served in small portions. No spices; no hot peppers; not even a proper amount of salt and pepper. We couldn't get over it. Whatever inferiority complexes we had about entering American homes were quickly cured by the poorly cooked food we were given to eat. Banana splits at some drugstore counter were nothing to sneer at; the tasteless, soggy white bread they served at home made no sense. When we wanted to eat well, we'd seek out a Hungarian or German restaurant in Yorkville or an Italian place down in the Village.

Of course, we always had the option of getting together with other Yugoslavs for some home-style food. However, there was a heavy price to pay. The talk made it difficult to enjoy the cuisine. Exiles usually imagine that theirs is a temporary situation. It was just a matter of days before communism collapsed and their homes and their lives would be restored to them just as they were. Nostalgia is big on the menu at such gatherings, and so is anger at how events turned out. My parents were tired of Balkan squabbles; they wanted a breather. Also, they didn't think there was a likelihood of ever going back. They turned out to be right. The Communists, thinly disguised as democrats, are still in charge at home and so is the old secret police.

To want to be an American, which I certainly desired, made us strangers even to our own kind. They eyed us suspiciously. Without the superiority one's own ethnic group readily provides, what do you have? It's terrible when collective sentiments one is born with begin to seem artificial, when one starts to suspect that one's exile is a great misfortune but also a terrific opportunity to get away from everything one has always secretly disliked about the people one grew up with.

I now understand the big choice we made without quite realizing that we were making it. We stopped seeing our fellow Yugoslavs. Already in those early days, I realized that America gave me an opportunity to stop playing the assigned roles that I inevitably had to play around my fellow Serbs. All that deferring to tradition, clannishness, and machismo, with their accompanying vocabularies, I happily gave up. Nor did the role of the professional exile, forever home-sick, forever misunderstood, attract me. Adventure lay elsewhere. America and the Americans were far more interesting to me and so was the anonymity that came with full-scale assimilation.

Actually, that's not entirely accurate. Many of my early friends were Italian, Jewish, Irish, and other immigrants. One of the great experiences of a city like New York was the exposure to so many other ways of life. The ideal of the times was, of course, the melting pot. Still, what did I know about the Blacks, Chinese, Cubans, Lebanese, Hungarians, Russians, Sicilians, before I lived in New York? There is no school as good as the life that takes you one day from a Hungarian butcher on Second Avenue, to an Irish bar in Chelsea, an Italian coffee shop on Macdougal Street, and a jazz club off Sheridan Square in the

company of a young woman who hails from Texas.
No wonder nationalists of all stripes hate cities. It's
hard to remain the faithful and obedient son of your
own clan when so many other attractive options offer
themselves. One has to be a fool or a hypocrite to sing
the praises of one's native customs to the exclusion of
every other, after one has lived in New York City. The
cities are, indeed, agreeably corrupting. They produce free individuals and that, as every state and religious institution the world over will tell you, is an
unpardonable heresy.

   If the choice, then, was between deepening
my own displacement and trying to belong, I made
my situation even more complicated by moving away
from home when I was eighteen. In other words,
exactly two years after I stepped off the 44th Street
pier, I found myself again adrift. My parents were not
getting along and life at home was most unpleasant,
so I had no alternative. I broke a few more ties I still
had to my old identity. I had no other relatives or
friends. I had no fixed address or purpose. There was
no question of college, because my parents were not
able to support me and my grades were not good
enough to get me a scholarship anywhere. But if you
think that I cried myself to sleep every night over my
predicament, you're wrong. It was one of the happi-
est times of my life. Finding a job and making ends
meet—as I discovered quickly—was very easy. Both in
Chicago and New York, I could find decent work in a
matter of hours. I did everything from being a mail

clerk at a newspaper to selling shirts in a department store. I worked in several offices as a bookkeeper. I met all kinds of interesting men and women. Best of all, I felt safe in this country from the persecutions we were accustomed to, and that was more than enough to make a young man permanently cheerful.

In the meantime, there were Charlie Parker, Thelonious Monk, Billie Holiday, Bessie Smith, Duke Ellington, the Five Spot, Birdland, rhythm and blues, country music, film noir, Scott Fitzgerald, Wallace Stevens, William Carlos Williams and the entire New Directions list, the Gotham Book Mart, MoMA, Willem de Kooning, Jackson Pollock, *Partisan Review*, the Brooklyn Dodgers, the Yankees, boxing at Madison Square Garden, "The Honeymooners," Sid Caesar, "I Love Lucy," and literally hundreds of other things to learn about. I was astonished to encounter other recent arrivals who had little or no interest in any of this.

To fall in love with a country or another human being requires some gullibility, and I had plenty to spare. It took me at least fifteen years to appreciate the full extent of our political corruption and to see the problems and injustices this country is faced with. Early on, I was living a version of the American Dream, ignorant of the simple fact that a white boy with an accent is more readily employable than a person of color. There has always been a kind of see-no-evil, let's-pretend demeanor about this country. It needs fresh supplies of true believers to keep it going, and that's what I was. In addition, there was the generosity that I and so many others found here. Every cliche about getting a second chance and reinventing oneself turned out to be true. It gave one confidence—America did that. Who could resist that sudden burst of optimism? I could not.

The clearest proof I had that I've become "an American" came to me in 1962 when I found myself in the U.S. Army in Europe, first in Germany and then in France. The little towns and small cities with their closely knit, insular societies frightened me. It was very pleasant to dine in one of the fine restaurants in Nancy or Colmar, but the silence of the streets after eight o'clock in the evening gave me the creeps: closed shutters, locked doors, lights out almost everywhere. I could well imagine what being a refugee there would be like.

More recently, during the break-up of Yugoslavia, I reexperienced my estrangement from the old world. I found myself, for example, incapable of taking sides or seeing any attraction in being a nationalist. The advantage of the melting pot is that it undermines tribalism. One gains a distance from one's own national folly. Fashionable present-day multiculturalism with its naive calls for ethnic pride sounds to me like an attempt to restore me to precisely that state of mind my parents ran away from in Europe. The American identity is a strange concoction of cultures, but at its best it is a concoction prepared and cooked by each individual in his or her own kitchen. It ought not to

come in a package with a label and a fake list of whole-
some, all-natural ingredients.

There's an old Soviet poster picturing Comrade Lenin
standing on the planet earth holding a broom. He's
sweeping off "undesirable elements," men and women
easily identified by their clothes as belonging to the
bourgeoisie. That was us. For that very reason, every
project for betterment of humanity, every collectivist
ideology, no matter how chaste it sounds, terrifies me.
Barbarism, intolerance, and fanaticism have been the
by-products of all utopian projects in this century.
Infallible theories of history and human progress
brought about the most repellent forms of repression.
The noble-sounding attempt to make the whole of
society accept a particular worldview always leads,
sooner or later, to the slaughter of the innocents.

We, displaced persons, were caught between two
rival intellectual projects: fascism and communism.
Our persecution was justified because we lagged in
our understanding of the laws of history. We stood in
the way, and so our misfortune was unavoidable and
not to be greatly regretted. This harsh view, as we
know, had the enthusiastic support of many of the
leading writers and intellectuals in Europe. The violence and injustice may have been regrettable, but
were in the service of messianic hopes for future happiness. The political writings of the times—both on

the left and the right—consist of endless justifications for inflicting death and suffering on the innocent.

If you think I'm exaggerating, consider this. While we stood in lines at the Prefecture, Sartre, Aragon, de Beauvoir, and their kind were dining in style or attending some gala at the Russian or Yugoslav embassy, celebrating Stalin's or Tito's birthday. In this century, the executioners' best friends have often turned out to be writers and intellectuals. The last remaining myth of our age is the myth of the intellectual's integrity and independence. The true enemy continues to be—to return to what I said at the very beginning—the innocent bystander. Or, more precisely, the antagonist has always been the individual conscience. It's that part of ourselves that remains stubbornly suspicious of mass enthusiasms, the one that makes us sleep badly at night. At 3 a.m., the proposed means that are justified by the lofty ends look pretty nasty. For the "lunatics of one idea," as Wallace Stevens called them, that has always been the supreme obstacle on the way to Utopia. Millions perished or lost everything while huge intellectual and military efforts were being made to obliterate and circumvent the conscience of countless human beings.

Speaking as one of the laboratory animals used in a series of famous historical experiments, I'd say I ended up, for better or for worse, with a clearer idea of how the world works—and that's no small matter. I prefer that solitary knowledge to the jubilation of the masses in Red Square or at some Nuremberg rally. I have a firm conviction that the ideologues on the left and on the right are interchangeable. I have a contempt for all shepherd-and-flock theories, all euphorias of thinking the same thought with hundreds of others, all preaching and moralizing in art and literature. Besides, I am a poet, the kind they call a lyric poet. A lyric poem is the voice of a single human being taking stock of his or her own existence. If it works, we speak of its "originality," meaning it is without precedent, it doesn't fit preconceived notions. The poem is both a part of history and outside its domain. That is its beauty and its hope. A poet is a member of that minority that refuses to be part of any official minority, because a poet knows what it is to belong among those walking in broad daylight, as well as among those hiding behind closed shutters.

ACKNOWLEDGMENTS

The editor would like to thank The New York Public Library for making this book possible, in particular its President, Paul LeClerc, with whom the idea of a lecture series on exile was born, Catherine Dunn, whose encouragement and advice always came at the right moment, David Cronin and Pamela Leo who organized the lecture series "Letters of Transit" on which this book is based, Karen Van Westering who championed its publication, and Anne Skillion whose unflagging and meticulous devotion to this book was a source of enduring support and great joy.

About the Authors

ANDRÉ ACIMAN is the author of *Out of Egypt: A Memoir.* He was born in Alexandria and lived in Egypt, Italy, and France. Educated at Harvard, he teaches at Bard College. He has written for *The New York Times, The New Yorker, The New Republic, The New York Review of Books,* and *Commentary,* and is the recipient of a Whiting Writers' Award and a Guggenheim Fellowship. He is currently working on a novel entitled *Over the Footbridge.*

EVA HOFFMAN was born in Kraków, Poland, and immigrated to Vancouver, Canada, at the age of thirteen. Educated at Harvard, she worked at *The New York Times* and has written widely on cultural and political subjects. She is the author of the memoir *Lost in Translation: A Life in a New Language,* for which she received the Academy of American Arts and Letters Jean Stein Award, and *Exit into History: A Journey Through the New Eastern Europe.* She has received a Whiting Writer's Award and a Guggenheim Fellowship. Her most recent book, *Shtetl*, was published in 1997, and received the Bronislaw Malinowski Social Science Award from the Polish Institute of Arts and Sciences.

BHARATI MUKHERJEE is the author of *The Middleman and Other Stories*, which won the National Book Critics' Circle Award, *Jasmine, The Holder of the World*, and most recently the novel *Leave It to Me*. She is the co-author with her husband, Clark Blaise, of *Days and Nights in Calcutta*, a journal of their year-long visit to India, and *The Sorrow and the Terror*. She is Professor of English at the University of California, Berkeley.

EDWARD W. SAID is University Professor of English and Comparative Literature at Columbia University and an influential cultural critic, political commentator, and writer on music. Born in Jerusalem, he left Palestine during the turmoil that led up to the creation of the state of Israel. His books include *Orientalism, The Question of Palestine, Musical Elaborations*, and *Culture and Imperialism*.

CHARLES SIMIC is a highly regarded poet, translator, and teacher. A native of Yugoslavia, he spent his formative years in Belgrade during World War II, immigrating to the United States when he was sixteen. He has won numerous awards including the prestigious MacArthur Foundation genius grant and the Pulitzer Prize in Poetry for *The World Doesn't End*. He is Professor of English at the University of New Hampshire.

www.ingramcontent.com/pod-product-compliance
Lightning Source LLC
Jackson TN
JSHW011939131224
75386JS00041B/1466

* 9 7 8 1 5 6 5 8 4 6 0 7 4 *